Passing It On

Investing In Lives

"From Grandpa With Love"

ISBN: 1502734788
ISBN 13: 9781502734785
Library of Congress Control Number: 2014918021
CreateSpace Independent Publishing Platform
North Charleston, South Carolina

A Collection of Later-in-Life Writings

"From Grandpa With Love"

Volume V

Even when I am old and gray, do not forsake me, O God,
till I declare your power to the next generation,
your might to all who are to come.
(Psalm 71:18)

Passing It On

This is last of a series of five *"From Grandpa With Love"* books that consolidate for publication many of the booklets I have been writing over the past 35 years to pass on what God was teaching me about life.

We opened the series with an overview of life, entitled *Four Generations: A Journey Through Life.* The next three volumes (*Faith, Marriage,* and *Vocation)* dealt with a trio of lifetime decisions we discussed briefly in *Four Generations* as follows:

> As I look back across my life, I see three principal life-time decisions and three important decision times...The three decisions concern our *Faith,* our *Marriage,* and our *Vocation.* Some have referred to these as our *Master,* our *Mate,* and our *Mission.* The three decision times usually seem to occur toward the end of each generation as we prepare to enter the next season of our lives.

This final book, *Passing It On*, discusses the age-old opportunity we have to invest in others what we have experienced and learned during our own journey through life..

Once more I say, "*Thank You.*" How grateful I am to the Lord and all those He has used to teach me, help me, and contribute to whatever I have written.

To God Be the Glory!

From Grandpa With Love

Marvin J. Martin
Wichita, Kansas
2015

Contents

Part I

What Am I Missing?

It is not good to have zeal without knowledge,
nor to be hasty and miss the way.
(Proverbs 19:2)

What Am I Missing?

1991

Recently, a young man who had been working in the corporate world for a few years asked:

"What am I missing?"

It reminded me of my own earlier years when it became obvious to me that the things of this world were not enough. I recall asking at that time a similar question:

"Is this all there is?"

It wasn't until several years later, when I finally accepted Jesus Jesus—not only as my nominal Savior but also as the actual Lord of my life—that God began to reveal a much deeper dimension of life than I had ever known.

I empathized greatly with this young man who was just beginning to enter the generation of this life that I was now completing some forty years later. I am sure that his life will have many differences from mine. However, there probably will also be many similarities. James Newby, at the close of his biography of Elton Trueblood, recognized the value of discussing the road ahead with older travelers as he quoted from a conversation between Socrates and Cephalus in Plato's *Republic*:

Socrates is reported as saying,
"There is nothing which for my part I like better, Cephalus,
than conversing with aged men;
for I regard them as travelers
who have gone on a journey which I too may have to go,
and of whom I ought to inquire whether the way
is smooth and easy, or rugged and difficult..."

I decided, therefore, to summarize and reduce to writing some of the major conclusions I have reached in the hope that it may help someone else as they travel through life. Listed below are ten principles that I encourage the reader to seriously consider not missing in order to receive as much as possible all the wonderful life God has for you.

Chapter 1

The Presence of God

I believe the most important fact in life is the presence of God. The first question God asked mankind (Adam) was:

> *Where are you?*
> (Genesis 3:9)

God asked the question because Adam had tried to hide from God after Adam had sinned by disobeying God and eating the forbidden apple (Genesis 3:1–8). Since then we have all tended to sin and turn away from God (Romans 3:23). This is deadly. I encourage you always to walk in the presence of God no matter where it may lead you and even though the road ahead seems hard.

Moses indicated his need for God's presence as he contemplated the overwhelming assignment God had given to him to lead the Israelites away from Egypt:

> *Moses said to the Lord, "You have been telling me,*
> *'Lead these people,' but you have not let me know*
> *whom you will send with me.*
> *You have said, 'I know you by name*
> *and you have found favor with me.'*
> *If you are pleased with me, teach me your ways*
> *so I may know you and continue to find favor with you.*
> *Remember that this nation is your people."*

> *The Lord replied, "My Presence will go with you,*
> *and I will give you rest."*
> *Then Moses said to him, "If your Presence*
> *does not go with us,*
> *do not send us up from here."*
> (Exodus 33:12–15)

Jonah tried (unsuccessfully) to run from God when he was told to go and preach to the wicked city of Nineveh. God, in His mercy, didn't allow Jonah to leave His Presence and gave Jonah a second chance after saving him through a great fish (Jonah 1–3; Matthew 12:39–41).

David, after his terrible acts of adultery with Bathsheba and having her husband Uriah treacherously killed, cried out to God in his "penitent's psalm":

> *Do not cast me from your presence...*
> (Psalm 51:11)

Jesus understood our great need for God's presence and promised His disciples as He prepared to leave them:

> *And I will ask the Father, and he will give you another Counselor*
> *to be with you forever—the Spirit of truth. The world cannot accept*
> *him, because it neither sees him nor knows him. But you know him,*
> *for he lives with you and will be in you. I will not leave you as*
> *orphans; I will come to you. Before long, the world will not see me*
> *anymore, but you will see me. Because I live, you also will live.*

On that day you will realize that I am in my Father,
and you are in me, and I am in you.
(John 14:16–20)

I will never forget the day that I became acutely aware of the presence of God in my life. I was driving alone through the Flint Hills of Kansas and meditating from this part of the Book of John. I came to John 14:23 in which Jesus said:

If anyone loves me, he will obey my teaching.
My Father will love him,
and we will come to him and make our home with him.

Suddenly, it overwhelmed me as I realized that God's Spirit truly was in my heart!

That realization has continued since that day. Not with the same emotional intensity, but with a quiet certitude that I am not alone and that God is present wherever I may be. When temptations arise and Satan attempts to control our lives, we need to walk even closer to God. As James says:

Submit yourselves, then, to God.
Resist the devil, and he will flee from you.
Come near to God and he will come near to you.
(James 4:7–8a)

When storms and problems seem to engulf us, the answer is the presence of God. Then we can say with Paul:

> *For I am convinced that neither death nor life,*
> *neither angels nor demons, neither the present*
> *nor the future, nor any powers, neither height nor depth,*
> *nor anything else in all creation,*
> *will be able to separate us from the love of God*
> *that is in Christ Jesus our Lord.*
> (Romans 8:38–39)

Perhaps the following poem, written in 1972, will be helpful for those who find rhythm and cadence an enjoyable aid to understanding and remembering.

Presence

The Lord spoke to Moses,
as a man speaks to his friend,
"Go, and lead the people
into a 'Milk and Honey' Land."

Moses asked the Lord,
"Please show me now thy ways."
He pleaded with God for guidance,
for vision through the haze.

God then gave to Moses,
the answer to his quest:
"My Presence will go with you,
and I will give you rest."

So when you look for answers
and when you feel the test,
Ask God's Presence to go with you,
and He will give you rest.

Chapter 2

The Word and Wisdom of God

The first question in the Bible related to God's Word. He had told Adam not to eat of one tree in the perfect paradise of Eden. But the Devil tempted Adam's wife, Eve, by asking:

> *Did God really say...?*
> (Genesis 3:1)

And then convinced her to doubt what God had said and to believe that he, Satan, offered the truth.

This has been the Devil's way ever since the Garden of Eden—to try to discredit God's Word. However, both the Old and New Testaments make it clear that God's Word is true. For example, the Prophet Isaiah, in announcing the Word of the Lord, said:

> *I, the Lord, speak the truth; I declare what is right.*
> (Isaiah 45:19b)

Jesus, on the night before He was betrayed, echoed this same conclusion as He prayed to His Father in Heaven:

> *...your word is truth.*
> (John 17:17b)

In a more personal way, Jesus made it clear that He was the Truth as He stated:

I am the way, and the truth and the life.
No one comes to the Father except through me.
(John 14:6)

He also joined Himself and His teachings with truth as He told the Jews who believed in Him:

If you hold to my teaching, you are really my disciples.
Then you will know the truth,
and the truth will set you free.
(John 8:31b–32)

God has given us a guidebook for life in the Bible. The Psalmist said:

How can a young man keep his way pure?
By living according to your word…
I have hidden your word in my heart
that I might not sin against you.
(Psalm 119:9, 11)

The Apostle Paul told his young associate, Timothy:

All Scripture is God-breathed and is useful
for teaching, rebuking, correcting and training in righteousness,
so that the man of God may be thoroughly equipped
for every good work.
(2 Timothy 3:16–17)

God's Word tells us how the world began, how it will end, and how we should live in the meantime. Man's laws and books are helpful.

However, they are fallible because man is fallible, and they also change and vary from time to time and from place to place.

By contrast, the Word of God in the small, concise Book we call the Bible holds the perfect, unchanging, reliable truth. I encourage you to make a habit of reading God's Word daily. This is a habit that can only be acquired by careful discipline. I found that I needed to set a specific time and place to be alone with God for prayer and His Word, or they would be crowded out by the cares and delights of everyday life. For me, the morning is best. It seems that I function better if I obtain both physical exercise and spiritual exercise at the beginning of the day, keeping in mind the admonition:

Have nothing to do with godless myths and old wives' tales; rather,
train yourself to be godly. For physical training is of some value,
but godliness has value for all things,
holding promise for both the present life and the life to come.
(1 Timothy 4:7–8)

Most of us find that both physical and spiritual exercises are difficult to maintain. Many years ago, a man told me that he could feel Satan tug at him each morning to pick up the newspaper and read it first. If he allowed that to happen before he spent time with God, it often deflected his course for the rest of the day. I have often had the same temptation. I find I need to spend time with God first, and then I can comfortably proceed on to breakfast and the news of the world.

I have found repeatedly that God speaks to me from these daily times with Him by giving me answers to problems I am encountering as I travel on a regular course through the Bible each year. For variety and new insights, a different translation is stimulating and helpful.

In addition to simply reading the Bible, I encourage you to get to know it so well that it is your friend. Memorize the names of the books of the Bible and understand what each of them is saying to us. Study the commands and biblical illustrations to find answers to your problems. Make it a practice to memorize key passages and to meditate and let the Scriptures soak deeply into your mind and heart so that they are available when you need them. Then apply what you learn so it will go well with you. Remember, Jesus cautioned at the conclusion of His great Sermon on the Mount:

Therefore everyone who hears these words of mine
and puts them into practice
is like a wise man who built his house on the rock.
The rain came down,
the streams rose, and
the winds blew and beat against that house;
yet it did not fall, because it had its foundation on the rock.
But everyone who hears these words of mine
and does not put them into practice is like a foolish man
who built his house on sand.
The rain came down, the streams rose,
and the winds blew and beat against that house,
and it fell with a great crash.
(Matthew 7:24–27)

Chapter 3

The Gifts of God

God has given us not only *physical* life, but because of His love for us, He has also offered us *eternal* life as well:

> *For God so loved the world*
> *that he gave his one and only Son,*
> *that whoever believes in him shall not perish*
> *but have eternal life.*
> (John 3:16)

Since God gives us eternal life, He will also supply all our other needs:

> *He who did not spare his own Son,*
> *but gave him up for us all—*
> *how will he not also, along with him,*
> *graciously give us all things?*
> (Romans 8:32)

However, we have to accept these gifts before we can enjoy them. Some folks won't receive God's gifts—even including the gift of His Son. For example:

> *He came to that which was his own,*
> *but his own did not receive him.*
> *Yet to all who received him,*

to those who believed in his name,
he gave the right to become children of God...
(John 1:11–12)

Once we accept the gift of eternal life, the Holy Spirit also gives us spiritual gifts to carry out our roles in life.

The Apostle Paul warns us:

Now about spiritual gifts, brothers,
I do not want you to be ignorant.
(1 Corinthians 12:1)

However, it has been my experience that many Christians lead a much less vital and fruitful life than they could have enjoyed because they have never discovered and begun to use the spiritual gifts God has given them (Romans 12:6–8; 1 Corinthians 12–14; Ephesians 4:7–16; 1 Peter 4:10–11). Understanding and using these gifts not only enables us to do the work God has planned for us, but often it also helps us to understand why others, including our spouses, think and act as they do.

After I had studied about spiritual gifts for some time, a spiritual mentor began to tell me that I probably had the gift of "mercy." But I asked myself, "How could that be? I am a labor law attorney. The gift of mercy will surely ruin my image and my business."

Finally, however, I submitted to God, and as an act of the will, I accepted this gift that God had offered to me. When that happened and I began to apply it, I realized it was right for me. The gift of mercy let me know where strengths and weaknesses of others were. While this gift could be abused by exploiting the weakness of others in a destructive manner, it also could be of great constructive help when used to heal, not to hurt. It allows us to sense tension in a group so we can then seek ways to bring about reconciliation. Instead of destroying my labor law practice, it ultimately allowed harmony and healing to take place instead of discord and defeat.

I don't know what physical and spiritual gift(s) God has given you. I do know that the Bible says God "wants all men to be saved and to come to a knowledge of truth" (1 Timothy 2:4), but not everyone is willing (Matthew 23:37). However, if you will allow Him, He will "give you the desires of your heart" and supply all your needs (Psalm 37:4; Philippians 4:19). That includes every physical and spiritual gift we need to carry out the work He has for us to do.

Chapter 4

The Love of God

One of God's greatest gifts is His love for us. After Paul discusses spiritual gifts in 1 Corinthians 12, he concludes by saying:

> *And now I will show you the most excellent way.*
> (verse 31b)

He then writes for us the great chapter on love, 1 Corinthians 13, which we hear quoted so often. Interestingly, after every discussion of our spiritual gifts in Romans, Ephesians, and 1 Corinthians, there is a discourse on love, as if to make certain we understand that it is only through God's love that we can effectively carry out His work.

The Apostle John tells us that "love comes from God" and "God is love" (1 John 4:7–8). However, as we discussed before, we must receive each gift before it is truly ours. Somehow this seems especially difficult for modern, independent, assertive, self-reliant folks like us.

God wants to love us, but He often does it through people—and sometimes through people from whom we don't want to accept God's gift of love. I have found that receiving can be a humbling experience. I hope you won't let pride or independence cause you to miss God's love for you.

Also, don't miss out on distributing God's love to others. They go hand in hand. We receive, and then we distribute. This allows room in our lives to receive more love, which we can then pass on to others. Jesus, in answering the question about the greatest commandment in the law, stated:

> *"Love the Lord your God with all your heart and with all your soul*
> *and with all your mind."*
> *This is the first and greatest commandment.*
> *And the second is like it:*
> *"Love your neighbor as yourself."*
> (Matthew 22:37–39)

The Apostle John discusses this intertwining when he says:

> *We love because he first loved us.*
> *If anyone says, "I love God," yet hates his brother,*
> *he is a liar.*
> *For anyone who does not love his brother,*
> *whom he has seen, cannot love God,*
> *whom he has not seen.*
> *And he has given us this command:*
> *Whoever loves God must also love his brother.*
> (1 John 4:19–21)

This love is shown in many ways, but it is principally evident as we give ourselves up and serve others. Jesus demonstrated such love for His disciples as He physically and symbolically knelt down and washed their feet. Then He told them:

> *A new command I give you: Love one another.*
> *As I have loved you,*
> *so you must love one another.*

18

By this all men will know that you are my disciples,
if you love one another.
(John 13:34–35)

Many years later, the Apostle John again defined such love:

This is how we know what love is:
Jesus Christ laid down his life for us.
And we ought to lay down our lives for our brothers.
If anyone has material possessions and sees his brother in need
but has no pity on him,
how can the love of God be in him?
Dear children, let us not love with words or tongue
but with actions and in truth.
(1 John 3:16–18)

Chapter 5

The Work of God

Getting to do the work we like to do with people we enjoy and in a place we like to be is one of life's really great pearls. I believe God has prepared work for us to perform while we are here on earth. When Jesus was asked if He was king of the Jews, He responded:

> *...for this reason I was born...*
> (John 18:37)

The prophet Jeremiah had a similar understanding:

> *The word of the Lord came to me, saying,*
> *"Before I formed you in the womb I knew you,*
> *before you were born I set you apart;*
> *I appointed you as a prophet to the nations."*
> (Jeremiah 1:4–5)

Psalm 139:16 reflects this conclusion for each of us:

> *...your eyes saw my unformed body.*
> *All the days ordained for me*
> *were written in your book before one of them came to be.*

In the New Testament, Ephesians 2:10 says it this way:

> *For we are God's workmanship,*
> *created in Christ Jesus to do good works,*
> *which God prepared in advance for us to do.*

I don't think it is so much a question of asking God to bless the work we choose to do, as it is to discover the work God has for us and then to enjoy God's blessings upon others and ourselves as we carry out this work in a Godly way (Colossians 3:23–24).

Moses, in Psalm 90:17, says it this way:

> *May the favor of the Lord our God rest upon us;*
> *establish the work of our hands for us—*
> *yes, establish the work of our hands.*

There is great joy in work. The ground was cursed in Genesis 3:17, but work was never cursed. Working with God predates the Fall, as shown by the fact that God put man in the Garden of Eden "to work it and take care of it" (Genesis 2:15). Work is a beautiful (and major) part of existence. The writer of Ecclesiastes repeatedly explains it is not the wealth and possessions we receive from work that we ultimately enjoy, since we never receive enough and end up having to leave whatever we have...

> *to the one who comes after me. And who knows*
> *whether he will be a wise man or a fool?*
> (Ecclesiastes 2:18b–19a)

Instead, it is the toil itself and the attendant pleasures of eating and drinking each day that are rewards in themselves. As Ecclesiastes says:

> *So I commend the enjoyment of life,*
> *because nothing is better for a man under the sun*
> *than to eat and drink and be glad.*
> *Then joy will accompany him in his work*

all the days of the life God has given him under the sun.
(Ecclesiastes 8:15; Ecclesiastes 2:24, 5:18–20)

It is a balancing act to know how much moneymaking work, how much recreation, how much family time, and how much time for others should take place. Here, we need the counsel of the Bible and Godly Christians, but it can be done.

I truly hope you will find work is not drudgery (keeping in mind that the joy of all beautiful babies is tempered by the reality of dirty diapers) and that you will feel that you, your family, and those you serve are all blessed by the work you do. There are four questions that I have found to be very helpful in determining the work we are to do:

- What do you want (like) to do?
- What do others *repeatedly* ask you to do?
- What bears good fruit when you do it?
- What bugs (i.e., bothers) you that isn't being done?

There are many, of course, who patiently and faithfully support themselves and their families by doing work that does not stimulate them. They are bound to their jobs because of other factors— e.g., family or financial obligations. However, Paul points out that even slaves who work "for the Lord" will ultimately be rewarded (Colossians 3:22–24).

Some work is done by words and some by works, but both should be service for God. As the Apostle Peter says:

Each one should use whatever gift he has received
to serve others, faithfully administering God's grace
in its various forms.
If anyone speaks, he should do it as one speaking the very words of God.
If anyone serves, he should do it with the strength God provides,
so that in all things God may be praised through Jesus Christ.
To him be the glory and the power for ever and ever.
Amen.
(1 Peter 4:10–11)

Those who are able to serve (minister) for God in the market-place are sorely needed as examples. It is hard, but not impossible, and it is very important. Paul states:

For you yourselves know how you ought to follow our example.
We were not idle when we were with you,
nor did we eat anyone's food without paying for it.
On the contrary, we worked night and day, laboring and toiling
so that we would not be a burden to any of you.
We did this, not because we do not have the right to such help,
but in order to make ourselves a model for you to follow.
For even when we were with you, we gave you this rule:
"If a man will not work, he shall not eat."
(2 Thessalonians 3:7–10)

While both men and women can work in the marketplace, only women can be mothers. I encourage wives, therefore, to consider carefully this special and unique work if you are called to marriage and God offers you this privilege.

It's a constant effort to know where God wants us to expend ourselves. It requires praying, being in the Word, receiving Godly counsel, using common sense, and understanding and applying our gifts, experience, and training. But all of us should be open to the guidance of the Holy Spirit. Several years ago, an older Christian told me that he was contemplating what God would have him do with his life when a Christian mentor said to him, "I think the Holy Spirit is doing something over in Europe. Why don't you go over and see if you can get in on it?" It was almost thirty years later that I heard this story, and the intervening years had been rich with blessings as this man ministered for Christ in that part of the world.

While we need the physical results of our labor to sustain life, this is not the ultimate goal of our work. Instead, Jesus tells us:

Do not work for food that spoils, but for food that endures to eternal life,
which the Son of Man will give you.
On him God the Father has placed his seal of approval.
(John 6:27)

When the audience asked Jesus:

What must we do to do the works God requires?
Jesus answered, "The work of God is this:
to believe in the one he has sent."
(John 6:28–29)

24

As we walk with God and believe in Jesus, we will see the work we are to do, keeping in mind that our goal is not so much to work for God as to allow God to work through us. Then we, like Paul, can say:

We proclaim him, admonishing and teaching everyone
with all wisdom, so that we may present everyone perfect in Christ.
To this end I labor, struggling with all his energy,
which so powerfully works in me.
(Colossians 1:28–29)

Chapter 6

The Peace of God

We live in a stress-filled world. Demands from all quarters can cause us to experience great anxiety. In retrospect, I believe much of my own anxiety (which has included both fear and anger) has come from being self-centered, trying to have my own way, and trying to protect myself. In short, I find there is a direct relationship between anxiety and concentration on self.

There are a number of biblical principles that have helped me in combating stress and appropriating the peace of God in my life.

Vaya Con Dios
The first is to concentrate on going with God, rather than asking Him to go with me. The Apostle Paul in Philippians 4:4–10 outlines the following steps for us to follow:

Rejoice (verses 4–6a). Rejoice in God and the knowledge of His presence. Put away anxiety as an act of the will.

Pray (verse 6b). Pray about everything rather than trying to take care of some matters ourselves and giving others to God for Him to handle. In this way, we can have confidence that God is in control of everything that may occur.

Give Thanks (verse 6b). Giving thanks in advance, at the very time we pray, reflects our total confidence that God has heard us and that the matters about which we have prayed are in His all-knowing and all-caring hands.

Think Positively (verse 8). Exchange all the critical, negative, fearful, and offensive thoughts for positive ones, and then keep our minds centered on these.

Act Right (verse 9). Finally, we must act right by following Godly models, which are provided in the Bible and by Godly people.

Live With A Margin

If you live with "a little gas in the tank and a little money in the bank," it makes life so much easier. Much of our anxiety and stress comes from having no margin when emergencies or opportunities arise. It has always saddened me when I find that I missed an appointment because I didn't start early enough or couldn't make an investment or gift because I hadn't set money aside. The habit of living with a margin requires self-discipline, but the rewards are enormous. This practice is particularly significant when we come to the place in life when we can no longer work to support ourselves and those for whom we provide. Jesus' parable of the ten virgins and their lamps in Matthew 25:1–13 is a good illustration of this principle.

Use the Rhythms of Life

God has established night and day, a day of rest each week, the yearly seasons, and chapters in our lives (Genesis 8:22; Exodus 20:8–10; Numbers 8:23–26). If we try to work night and day, seven days a week, summer and winter, all the years of our lives, we wear out and often become anxious. However, if we will follow God's principles of regular patterns of daily and weekly rest, together with vacations and recognition of our limitations as we travel through life, they will provide balance and rhythm, which will enhance our lives.

As one cartoon stated, "If you can do at 65 what you were doing at 25, then you weren't doing much at 25!" But, conversely, those at 25 have not yet had many experiences, which God will use to mature them into the people He has designed them to be. As Ecclesiastes 3:11a stated:

> *He has made everything beautiful in its time.*

Recognize Physical Signals
Proverbs 14:30 says:

> *A heart at peace gives life to the body,*
> *but envy rots the bones.*

Ulcers, backaches, headaches, and other ailments are now often accepted as being related to stress. Watch for any physical signals that God graciously provides to warn us that we are overstressing our lives.

Live Grace, Then Works
The Book of Luke tells the following story:

> *As Jesus and his disciples were on their way, he came to a village*
> *where a woman named Martha opened her home to him.*
> *She had a sister called Mary, who sat at the Lord's feet*
> *listening to what he said.*
> *But Martha was distracted by all the preparations that had to be made.*
> *She came to him and asked, "Lord, don't you care that my sister*
> *has left me to do the work by myself?*
> *Tell her to help me!"*
> *"Martha, Martha," the Lord answered, "you are worried and upset*

about many things, but only one thing is needed.
Mary has chosen what is better, and it will not be taken away from her."
(Luke 10:38–42)

I find stress and anxieties are greatly diminished when I spend time with Jesus—and then do my work.

Accept Your Limitations

We all have certain gifts and qualities God has given to us (Psalm 139:13–16; 1 Corinthians 12). But none of us has everything. It is important that we find where we do well and then seek out others to act where we cannot. As one employer said to me, "I just look for good people and get out of their way."

Then Be Content

Contentment is an attitude that we develop based upon trust in God, rather than by acquiring worldly possessions or achieving worldly goals. When we trust God, we can say, like Paul:

...for I have learned to be content whatever the circumstances.
I know what it is to be in need, and I know what it is to have plenty.
I have learned the secret of being content
in any and every situation, whether well fed or hungry,
whether living in plenty or in want. I can do everything
through him who gives me strength.
(Philippians 4:11b–13)

Jesus assures us:

Peace I leave with you; my peace I give you.
(John 14:27a)

But He warns us that this will not be a worldly peace:

> *I do not give to you as the world gives.*
> *Do not let your hearts be troubled and do not be afraid.*
> (John 14:27b)

While it isn't always possible to live with peace around us, it is possible to live with the peace of God *within us*—if we follow Him and His principles.

Chapter 7

The Worship (Fear) of God

The Bible tells us repeatedly that we should fear God (Deuteronomy 6:13; Joshua 24:14; Psalm 33:8; Proverbs 1:7; Ecclesiastes 12:13; Luke 12:5; Revelation 14:7). But I have come to realize that it is a fear based not upon dread but rather upon respect and a desire to worship God. Unless we understand that God is perfect and holy and deserves our praise, we can come to ignore Him and ultimately try to be our own god.

The early Israelites learned to praise God. I find no better model for praise and worship of God than the last five Psalms, each of which lifts us up to God and begins and ends with:

Praise the Lord.

For me, music is an essential part of worship. Melodies and words, instruments and voices all combine to lift many of us closer to God.

Unfortunately, much of our worship is cultural. Thus, we kneel, sit, stand, raise our hands, clap, sing, dance, pray aloud, or refrain from any or all of these based largely upon our traditions. Some of us use chants from centuries ago, others sing hymns from the 18th and 19th centuries, and some lift their hearts to God through contemporary song and instrumentation.

Just as we need the whole counsel of God, so have I found profit in experiencing many forms of worship. The reverence of silence, the submission in kneeling, the drama of the spoken word, and the exultation and joy of singing, dancing, and clapping—when done unto God and not for public approval or effect—have all given me a closer sense of God and hopefully have been pleasing to Him.

In the final analysis, however, worship is not simply what we do during church service or in our own quiet time, but rather how we direct our total lives. The Apostle Paul urges us to see this totality as he states:

> *Therefore, I urge you, brothers, in view of God's mercy,*
> *to offer your bodies as living sacrifices, holy and pleasing to God*
> *this is your spiritual act of worship.*
> (Romans 12:1)

And the NIV Study Bible, in commenting on this passage, cautions:

> Not merely ritual activity,
> but the involvement of heart, mind, and will.
> (New International Version,
> Zondervan Bible Publishers)

There is also a significant effect on others when we worship. As we gather together on Sunday, as we erect church buildings that point toward Heaven, and as we publicly acknowledge our dependence upon our Creator through inscriptions in and upon our buildings and by prayer and acknowledgment of God in private and public writings, we honor Him, uplift ourselves, and impact for good the communities in which we live.

Chapter 8

The Grace of God

The law of God is beautiful and necessary. However, it is so perfect we cannot always understand it, and we do not always follow it. For this reason, we need the grace that comes through Jesus.

> *For the law was given through Moses;*
> *grace and truth came through Jesus Christ.*
> (John 1:17)

We are saved by God's grace and not because of our works (Ephesians 2:8–9). We also need to live by grace, as Jesus emphasized in His magnificent Sermon on the Mount:

> *So do not worry, saying, "What shall we eat?" or*
> *"What shall we drink?" or*
> *"What shall we wear?"*
> *For the pagans run after all these things,*
> *and your heavenly Father knows that you need them.*
> *But seek **first** his kingdom and his righteousness,*
> *and all these things will be given to you as well.*
> (Matthew 6:31–33; emphasis added)

There will always be great tension among law, grace, and works. We need them all. But somehow, grace seems to go against our modern, independent, rule-minded society.

For many years, I asked God to give me a grateful heart. I finally discovered this comes, at least in part, from accepting and living by God's grace. By contrast, bitterness seems to come into our spirit when we either refuse to accept the grace of God or to grant it to others.

All of us sin. It is only through God's grace and forgiveness that we are cleansed and made whole:

> *If we claim to be without sin, we deceive ourselves*
> *and the truth is not in us. If we confess our sins,*
> *he is faithful and just and will forgive us our sins*
> *and purify us from all unrighteousness.*
> (1 John 1:8–9)

When that happens, we are eternally grateful. But Jesus made it clear that we must extend this same grace and forgiveness to others:

> *For if you forgive men when they sin against you,*
> *your heavenly Father will also forgive you.*
> *But if you do not forgive men their sins,*
> *your Father will not forgive your sins.*
> (Matthew 6:14–15)

The parable of the servant who was forgiven a huge debt but who then refused to forgive someone who owed him a much smaller debt is a dramatic reminder of this great truth and its consequences (Matthew 18:21–35).

Chapter 9

The Kingdom of (Heaven) God

God is the Ruler of all (Isaiah 37:16). For now, however, He has allowed Satan to rule the earth (John 12:31; 16:11). When Jesus came and proclaimed the Kingdom of God on earth, He was rejected (John 1:11) and ultimately crucified by those whom He came to save. Listen as He explains to Pilate:

> *Jesus said, "My Kingdom is not of this world.*
> *If it were, my servants would fight to prevent my arrest by the Jews.*
> *But now my kingdom is from another place."*
> (John 18:36)

Those of us who acknowledge Jesus Christ as Lord are also called to live as aliens and exiles in this world:

> *Dear friends, I urge you,*
> *as aliens and strangers in the world,*
> *to abstain from sinful desires,*
> *which war against your soul.*
> (1 Peter 2:11)

We are called to be holy, i.e., set apart, and different from the world around us. Down through the centuries, this seems to begin with the issue of sexual purity. Paul warns in 1 Corinthians 6:18–20:

Flee from sexual immorality.
All other sins a man commits are outside his body,
but he who sins sexually sins against his own body.
Do you not know that your body
is a temple of the Holy Spirit, who is in you,
whom you have received from God?
You are not your own; you were bought at a price.
Therefore honor God with your body.

In Galatians 5:19–25, an extensive list of acts of our sinful nature are cataloged, again beginning with "sexual immorality, impurity, and debauchery." These passages make it clear that we must crucify our sinful nature in order to be a part of the Kingdom of God:

The acts of the sinful nature are obvious:
sexual immorality, impurity, and debauchery; idolatry and witchcraft;
hatred, discord, jealousy, fits of rage, selfish ambition, dissensions,
factions, and envy; drunkenness, orgies, and the like.
I warn you, as I did before, that those who live like this will not inherit
the kingdom of God.
But the fruit of the Spirit is love, joy, peace, patience, kindness,
goodness, faithfulness, gentleness, and self-control.
Against such things there is no law.
Those who belong to Christ Jesus have crucified the sinful nature
with its passions and desires.
Since we live by the Spirit, let us keep in step with the Spirit.

However, the Kingdom of Heaven is so valuable that it is worth whatever sacrifice we must make to obtain it.

The kingdom of heaven is like treasure hidden in a field.
When a man found it, he hid it again,
and then in his joy went and sold all he had and bought that field.
Again, the kingdom of heaven is like a merchant looking for fine pearls.
When he found one of great value,
he went away and sold everything he had and bought it.
(Matthew 13:44–46)

If we see ourselves as citizens of this Heavenly Kingdom, it often puts us in conflict with the world, just as it did Jesus. The Beatitudes show that those who would receive the Kingdom of God will evidence humility and submission and will likely suffer persecution as they proceed through life (Matthew 5:3,10).

Satan, as the ruler of this world, offers to us (as he did to Jesus) pleasure, possessions, and power (position) if we will abandon the Kingdom of God and follow Satan. He lures us as he did Jesus:

And he said to him,
"I will give you all their authority and splendor,
for it has been given to me, and I can give it to anyone I want to.
So if you worship me, it will all be yours."
(Luke 4:6–7)

The problem, of course, is that if we accept Satan's offer and spend our lives only pursuing the rewards of this world, we miss the Kingdom of (Heaven) God and all it offers to us for eternity.

Jesus repeatedly told us of the wonderful Kingdom of Heaven we can enjoy if we are loyal citizens of that Kingdom. Over and over again, He relates parables in the Gospels to help us to understand the importance of acknowledging the Kingdom of God as our eternal home. Eternity is a long time. How marvelous to enjoy the Kingdom of Heaven forever with our perfect Lord and His people.

Chapter 10

The People of God

As I look back over the years, it is increasingly apparent that my relationship with God and with His people has become the most important part of my life. We opened our discussion with our need for God's Presence. We now close it with this section concerning God's People. Here I refer to all people, whether or not they have received eternal life by accepting Jesus Christ as their Lord and Savior.

The Bible begins with the account of God's creation of the world. After each of the first items He created, God pronounced that it was "good." However, during the course of His creating, God announced a situation that He found was "not good." After creating one man, God said:

> *It is not good for the man to be alone.*
> *I will make a helper suitable for him.*
> (Genesis 2:18)

So He did. And through the joining of man and woman, He has provided people for every succeeding generation that we might know and enjoy one another.

We all crave companionship. Being alone can be awesome and frightening. I believe God places this desire for companionship in us to draw us first to Him and then to one another. While we need some space, we all need to be connected to God and to other human beings.

God reserves the deepest, most intimate companionship for those who become husbands and wives, and thereby "become one flesh" (Genesis 2:22–24). Although it is clear that not all individuals are to marry (in fact, Paul cautions against marriage under some circumstances in 1 Corinthians 7), if God does call you to marriage, I believe it can be the most wonderful of all earthly relationships.

While our deepest need and desire is for fellowship with God and then with our spouse (if we are married), we also crave companionship with others. God gives us the opportunity for such relationships in all directions. Extended family and friends can all become increasingly important as we grow older. Long-term relationships can grow dearer with the passing years. Don't let miles or time destroy your relationships with family and friends.

To give us a sense of belonging while allowing us to retain our individual uniqueness, God also created us as a part of His Body. The Apostle Paul repeatedly describes this separate yet oneness we have as brothers and sisters in Christ as he states:

> *The body is a unit, though it is made up of many parts;*
> *and though all its parts are many, they form one body.*
> *So it is with Christ...Now the body is not made up of one part*
> *but of many...As it is, there are many parts, but one body...*
> *If one part suffers, every part suffers with it;*
> *if one part is honored, every part rejoices with it.*
> *Now you are the body of Christ,*
> *and each one of you is a part of it.*
> (1 Corinthians 12:12, 14, 20, 26, 27)

We can enjoy this companionship through all avenues of church and parachurch groups and activities. Some of my deepest relationships have come from small Bible study groups, one-on-one discipleship, and two-by-two reach-outs to those who do not yet know Christ.

Many years ago, I said to a more mature Christian I had met, "I've been reading about Christian fellowship and I would like to know where I can get some!" He didn't laugh or send me away. Instead, we began a lifelong fellowship in Christ. I encourage you to consider some advice I was given early in my Christian walk, i.e., find some others who are more mature, some who are less mature, and some who are equally mature in Christ and spend time walking with them.

Since we all have to make the decision whether or not we will deny ourselves and become one with Christ, He obviously wants us to know and relate to all those around us, whether or not they have accepted Christ into their lives. As Paul stated:

I have become all things to all men
so that by all possible means I might save some.
(1 Corinthians 9:22b)

Here is one of Jesus' greatest hallmarks: that he reached out to all men and women everywhere. We have this same opportunity with all those in the sphere of relationships that God gives to each of us.

Many years ago, I unconsciously separated myself from people by work and activities. When it finally became apparent to me that God and other people were more important, I asked Him to help me to change. At first I spent time with others as an act of the will. But over the years, God has changed my heart. While it still requires effort, I now recognize and want the satisfaction that comes from companionship with others. Friendship is a marvelous gift—to receive and to give.

Conclusion

It isn't enough, of course, simply to know God's principles—we must also put them into practice. As James says:

Do not merely listen to the word, and so deceive yourselves.
Do what is says.
(James 1:22)

God has a wonderful, meaningful life planned for each of us, but we must reach for it. I encourage you, therefore, to spend your life living, loving, sharing, and being yourself with all the natural beauty, ability, and purpose that entails.

Don't sell out for short-term pleasure or success at the expense of your whole life, like Esau, who sold his birthright for a pot of stew (Genesis 25:29–34). Build good memories, not regrets. Build good relationships, not bitterness. Patiently plant and nurture love, wisdom, and goodness in life so you can enjoy a bountiful harvest at the close of your years, rather than dashed dreams and sadness for what might have been.

The Book of Ecclesiastes, that many believe was written by Solomon toward the close of his life, discusses the false hopes that we have in pursuing worldly pleasures, possessions, power, and position. Nine times he cautions us against the meaninglessness of "chasing the wind." Each of us receives our allotted time. If we spend it "chasing the wind," we do not have the time and energy to spend our lives in the fulfilling and meaningful way God had planned for us.

Don't forget that life rolls quickly by. As the poignant song in the musical *Fiddler on the Roof* says, "Sunrise, sunset, swiftly fly the years." When we were younger, I remember the generation ahead of us saying, "Where did it all go? We look around and suddenly we're old!" Now I hear *my* generation beginning to utter these same words.

My hope and prayer, therefore, for each of you, as for myself, is that we would increasingly follow the model of Paul, as he exclaimed with hope and determination:

> *Not that I have already obtained all this,*
> *or have already been made perfect,*
> *but I press on to take hold of that for which Christ Jesus took hold of me.*
> *Brothers, I do not consider myself yet to have taken hold of it.*
> *But one thing I do: Forgetting what is behind*
> *and straining toward what is ahead,*
> *I press on toward the goal to win the prize*
> *for which God has called me heavenward in Christ Jesus.*
> (Philippians 3:12–14)

Part II

From Grandpa With Love

Even when I am old and gray, do not forsake me, O God,
till I declare your power to the next generation,
your might to all who are to come.
(Psalm 71:18)

Preface

Circa 2000

This is a message from a grandfather who grew up in the Depression/World War II era (1925–1950) to his grandchildren's generation as they reach adulthood.

These remarks were first prepared for presentation to a group of college and university students at a Student Leadership Conference on Faith and Values, as we were transitioning from the 20th to the 21st centuries. It later was given to other young men and women in other locations. Except for minor editing, it is repeated here as we discussed it fifteen years ago.

I cautioned as I delivered this message, "Sooner or later, every person, every group, and every institution all come to the hard part of life." But I was certainly not prepared for how quickly it happened, and how vastly the world would change after terrorists crashed airliners into the World Trade Center in New York City and the Pentagon in Washington, DC, on September 11, 2001, just a little over a year later!

It makes me pray even more fervently for a deep and abiding faith for those who now face the troublesome years ahead.

From Grandpa With Love

From Grandpa With Love

As I look back on life, I find that we seem to live it in chapters or generations. For many of us, age 0 to 25 is a time when we "Learn." Age 25 to 50 is a time when we "Do." Age 50 to 75 is a time when we help others "Learn and Do." And age 75 onward is a time when most of us will "Finish" the race.

So we learn to play ball, then we play ball, and finally we coach others so they can play ball. We are children, then we become parents, and then we become grandparents. If we live long enough, we may become great-grandparents. Some of you may someday have that pleasure. Based on current life expectancy, many of you may live to be 90. So I encourage you to schedule your lives accordingly.

I urge you to expand your view of time. I have become convinced that in order to be mature and in order to lead, you must begin to look further into the past and also project your thinking further into the future. If you live only for the present, you are apt to be shallow and ineffective.

I was born in 1925. I will be 75 this year. I grew up in what has been described as the Depression/World War II generation. Age 7 to 12 for me was 1932 to 1937. We moved to a small acreage that we called "The Farm" in order to grow our own food. Sometimes I had the responsibility to milk the cows—the old-fashioned way, with a metal bucket and seated on a milking stool next to the cow. There were two common ways to make a milk stool. One was quick and easy: just nail two boards together like a *T* and sit on it, but you wobbled. The other way was harder: make a seat and put three legs under it. It took longer to make the stool, but you were more apt to safely finish your milking job.

Lots of things in life seem to be like that. For example, in government we have found that the three branches—Legislative, Executive, and Judicial—produce much a more stable government than relying only on one powerful head. Likewise, the Bible gives us God in Three Persons: the Father, the Son, and the Holy Spirit, whom we refer to as the "Trinity."

Following that pattern, let's link the three concepts of "Faith, Hope, and Love", and then relate all three of these to Time. And so you will know where we are headed, let me say that I believe "Faith" comes from the past, "Hope" is what draws us to the future, and "Love" is what we are to enjoy and distribute now and forever.

Faith

First, let's talk about faith. Faith is the foundation of all we do in our lives. It forms our belief system, and our actions flow from what we believe.

Developing Our Faith
I think we develop our faith, i.e., our belief system, based on what we see and hear and experience, both externally and internally. Growing up seems to be a time when we sort out these beliefs. First comes our home environment, then schools and other organizations, and ultimately, the whole world around us as well as

the spirit within us. These all have an impact on what we believe. That becomes our faith.

It is an evolving process. Usually, by the time we reach our teens, we have made some basic decisions about our faith. And by age 25, most of us seem to have adopted a belief system that we will consciously or unconsciously use during the coming years.

Where Do We Place Our Faith?
Some of us will place our faith primarily in ourselves. This is becoming more and more the norm in our individualistic society. Some will place their faith in others—perhaps in a great leader or an organization they want to follow. Some will put their faith in economics, others in government. Still others believe science is the ultimate answer. And others will choose God.

But for most of us, it seems to be some combination of these. As a result we can become double minded and unsure of what we believe.

I was this way for many years. As was probably true for you, I felt early in my life the pull of the world around me, and also an inside pull from God. I could plainly see the results of both, and I knew that both were real. And both were tugging at me.

But which one was to be the foundation of my life?

Do We Really Need God?
I wanted all the things in the world: its pleasures, success, and position. But I also wanted the peace, strength, and tranquility that God offered.

My struggle went on for many years. I attended Kansas University, married, completed Law School, and began to practice law. Both our family and law practice grew.

When times are good, it is easy to rely on ourselves and the institutions that support our society. In such an environment, it is tempting to say, "Who needs God?" In addition, when we are young, we often don't believe much can hurt us. That can be good to a degree, because it gives the confidence to proceed into the new, uncharted waters of the future. But sooner or later we find that is not enough. Simply relying on ourselves and the people and institutions around us seems to have a way of crumbling or dissolving when unseen disaster strikes.

It was my time in history to live as an adult from the close of World War II in 1945 to the present. During this time, parts of the world have prospered physically and materially beyond measure. This does encourage our faith in mankind. But underlying this peace, health, and material prosperity is a growing realization that these have often been accompanied by a decline in marriage, family life, and many moral values. In addition, our wars in other nations such as Korea, Vietnam, Iraq, and Kosovo—together with the seemingly endless conflicts (with their accompanying poverty, hurt, and misery) in Africa, Asia, Russia, and elsewhere—make it obvious that placing our faith only in mankind and his institutions will never be a permanent solution.

It is my belief that something more is needed. Faith must be placed in a higher power than mankind if it is to succeed long term.

Single-Minded Faith
For me it became a faith in the life and teaching of Jesus. In 1969, at age 44, I finally stopped my double-minded faith. I surrendered control of my life to God and accepted Jesus as divine. From that point on, my faith has been in Him.

It has made a difference beyond measure. My law practice had been concentrated in Labor matters involving union-company disputes. It was so controversial that our own office was bombed. I gradually discovered that if I would speak and act with courtesy and for the good of all concerned, I could often change the environment and end with agreements rather than strikes and work stoppages. Relationships with my wife and children improved greatly. And through it all, my own life began to change and become a time of joy rather than inner turmoil and conflict. These past thirty years have been the best of my life. Not always easy, but unbelievably rewarding.

When Should We Make a Decision About Our Faith?
Your generation now stands at the threshold of the 21st century. My generation's time is now history. The torch has been passed to you. Each of you also stands at the threshold of your own adult lives. Because of that, I can't urge you too strongly to make a decision about your faith—and do it quickly! Your lives will fly by more swiftly with each passing year, so don't wait.

How Can We Make a Decision About Our Faith?
I don't know where you will place your faith. But remember, you are staking not only your entire life but also eternity on your

belief system! Make the decision not on the desires of the moment, so when you look back at age 75, and on into eternity, you will be pleased with the choice you have made.

In order to make the best choice, I would encourage you to watch and study those who have gone before you. Not only those you know personally, but also those you discover through history and biographical information. Determine what their faith has produced for them and others. Ask yourselves the tough questions:

- Has it sustained them in the hard times as well as easy times?
- Has it produced good or evil around them?
- Has it brought about an inner, lasting, and joyful view of the present and also of eternity?

Then pray! Remember:

- Faith is a gift. Pray for it.
- Faith is gradual. Pray for it to increase.
- Faith overcomes fear. Pray for the courage to believe and act right during the hard times.

As one older man told me, "What I fed the most grew the most!" If you want faith in God, spend time with Him and what He has written through His people.

In the final analysis, faith deals with what we cannot see. That is why we call it faith. At some point I believe you find yourself in the position where you need to step out and place your faith in the unseen hand of God.

Hope

What Is Hope?

Now let's look at hope. While faith is built on what we have seen, heard, and experienced in the past, hope deals with what we want to happen in the future. The *American Heritage Dictionary* defines hope as "to entertain a wish for something with some expectation of fulfillment."

We all need hope. Without hope we become discouraged. If hope fades, the future begins to look grim and foreboding; but when we have hope we can become confident and upbeat. So we need to ask ourselves, "When and how do we get hope?"

The Bible says,

> *Now faith is being sure of what we hope for...*
> (Hebrews 11:1)

Thus, faith and hope seem to be intertwined. If my faith has been well placed and proved reliable in the past, then I will probably be confident of the future. But if my faith has been broken or shattered in the past, I likely will not be confident about the future, and I can become easily discouraged or frightened about what lies ahead.

Three Generations of Hope

Each generation has its unique battles to fight and mountains to climb. If we look only at what is going on around us in this world, it can cause us to gain or lose hope depending on how things are going at that particular time. Let me give you an example of what I mean by looking at three generations.

Generation I (1925 to 1950)
As a grandparent, I am two generations ahead of you. Let's call my age group Generation I. I was a teenager when World War II began in 1941. But I had hopes, just as you do. I hoped the Army Air Corps (as they were known in those days before we had the Air Force) would accept me into its cadet program. It did. I left for Basic Training in September 1943, at the age of 18 plus one month. I hoped I would earn my Navigator Wings. I did.

I hoped our B-29 crew would successfully complete our missions. The day the war ended in August 1945, we were over the Pacific Ocean headed back to our base on the island of Guam from the last air raid of the war.

Then, finally and most importantly to me, I hoped I would get back home safely to the United States. And I did. I arrived in the train station of my hometown on July 4, 1946—the day I always called my Independence Day!

By the time the young people of my generation reached age 25, they had seen an economic depression with its unemployment and bread lines. They had seen some governments use their power not for good, but rather to enslave and destroy millions, including Jews and Russian dissidents. And they had seen science used not to save lives, but rather to destroy them by the millions through all kinds of lethal devices, including firebombs and atomic holocausts.

At the close of World War II, General Douglas MacArthur, the commander of the Allied forces in the Pacific, signed the Japanese peace treaty on an American ship in Tokyo Bay. He then broadcast a message to the American people. Let me give you part of that message:

> "Today the guns are silent. A great tragedy is ended. A great victory has been won. The skies no longer rain death, and the seas bear only commerce. Men everywhere walk upright in the sunlight. The entire world is at peace. The holy mission has been completed. And in reporting this to you, the people, I speak for the thousands of silent lips, forever still among the jungles and the beaches and in the deep water of the Pacific, which have marked the way."

He concluded the broadcast with these solemn words:

> "We have had our last chance. If we do not now devise some greater and more equitable system, Armageddon will be at our door. The problem basically is theological and involves a spiritual recrudescence and improvement of human character that will synchronize with our almost matchless advances in science, art, literature, and all material and cultural developments of the past 2000 years. It must be of the spirit if we are to save the flesh."

At the conclusion of each great war, there seems to be a resurgence of hope that man has finally learned his lesson, and that future generations will now be able to enjoy the peace and prosperity we all so desperately want. This mood also prevailed after World War II. Again there was a great wave of hope. Formation of the United

Nations, steady improvements in economic conditions, and great advances in science all seemed to promise a new dawn of faith and hope that man would be able to get it right this time.

Most of my generation seemed to have this hope. I believe it was because our nation had successfully met some challenges in our brief past—so it gave us hope for the future. But it was a hope that was going to be seriously challenged over the next fifty years.

Generation II (1950 to 1975)
The late 1940s saw the beginning of a cold war with Russia, followed by the war in Korea and a series of new crises.

Our children (and your parents) were born during this time period. We'll call them Generation II. Most of them came of age during the deeply divided era of the 1960s and 1970s. Instead of victory in war, they watched our nation lick its wounds and withdraw from our misguided attempt to bring peace to Vietnam. Instead of constructive discourse, they saw the assassinations of three great leaders: President John F. Kennedy, his brother Robert Kennedy, and Martin Luther King Jr. Instead of unity they saw a myriad of groups clamoring for special rights for their particular constituents. Deep wounds stretched across the land.

Instead of breeding hope, this kind of atmosphere spawned distrust and discouragement. It was not conducive to hope for the future. In addition, the crisis of our own government caused by President Nixon's Watergate scandal, followed by runaway inflation, increased the anxiety about what the future might hold.

One result was that some in this generation seemed to lose faith in traditional ways, and they tried to substitute drugs and other short-term pleasures for long-term hope. But, interestingly, it led many others to a great spiritual revival.

Generation III (1975 to 2000)
Now, what about your generation—you who were born around 1975 or later? Let's call you Generation III. I am sure that some of you have already been severely tested as individuals as you have struggled with health, finances, family, or other difficult issues. For many of you, your faith is strong and your hope is bright. But as a generation, and as a group, you are largely untried. You have lived your years in one of the greatest, upbeat times in the history of our nation. You have grown up with economic prosperity beyond measure. You are accustomed to full employment and no trouble finding a job. The stock market is at an all-time high. Internet and telecommunication stocks have skyrocketed in value. Science seems to produce more and more extraordinary wonders. And the only wars most of you have known were far away and quickly won—for example, the ground troops in the Gulf War were able to report victory in a matter of days or hours rather than in months or years!

Everlasting Hope
But life is not always so kind. When you come to the year 2050 and look back on the fifty years we are entering, I expect you, too, will be able to tell your grandchildren about your World War, or economic collapse, or terrorism, or plagues, or some other unexpected and totally unwanted circumstances. Let me warn you, if you put your faith only in people or institutions

during such widespread crises, your capacity for hope will likely get severely damaged.

If you are fortunate to live through another era like World War II with its victory and unity—fine. But those historical times usually come along only once in several generations. In between we have to learn to have faith and hope in something that is more reliable than winning a war or overcoming an economic depression. We need something that will see us through the bad times of discord, conflict, and defeat, not just in the times when we win competitive races.

Sooner or later, every person, every group, and every institution all come to the hard part of life. Whether we are going to have hope—real, everlasting hope—during these difficult times will be determined by where our faith is based.

I urge you, of course, to have faith in yourselves and those around you—and in the institutions of family, church, workplace, and government. These are all necessary and desirable parts of our lives. But when the hard times come, when these people and/ or institutions are unable to help, be sure you have a faith that undergirds all the others.

A Hope For the Future
You stand at the dawn of a new century and a new millennium, and also at the beginning of the most productive years of your lives. By contrast, I am coming to the end of my journey. Yet never have I had more hope or more optimism about the future. I want to continue to be that way. I want to be like the 90-year-old

grandmother who bought a new carpet and demanded a 15-year guarantee!

But my hope and optimism are not because I believe my generation, or your parent's generation, or your generation have or will solve all the world's problems and bring us and future generations eternal peace, health, and prosperity.

No! My hope and optimism are because I now realize after all these years that there are new challenges in every generation. But a deep and abiding faith in God can give you, just as it has given countless others throughout the ages, an unending and ever-present hope and the ability to persevere and move through every situation you may ever have to face!

Love

What Is Love?
Finally, let's talk about love, the third and last part of our trilogy. Love is one of the simplest, yet most complex, words in our language. There is romantic love, brotherly love, and spiritual love. We love our homes, our nation, and our french fries. We love a good movie or book, and we are told to "love God."

One friend recently asked a group of us, "What does love really mean, and how can we do it?"

We don't have time here for a detailed and involved discussion, but let's see if we can at least make a few observations and suggestions that may help.

1 Corinthians 13, one of the great Biblical chapters about love, ends with a phrase that is the basis for our conversation. I'm sure it is familiar to many of you:

> *And now these three remain: faith, hope, and love.*
> *But the greatest of these is love.*

I believe faith gives us a foundation for life, hope gives us a desire for life, and love gives us a way of life.

Which Way of Life Shall We Choose?
Each of us must decide the road we will travel during the years we are granted. Jesus, at the close of His great Sermon on the Mount, talks about two roads. We can choose the popular road and devote our time and energies to satisfy our own desires by seeking wealth, personal pleasure, or fame. One famous man, King Solomon, who wrote a book called Ecclesiastes in which he talks repeatedly about trying that road, said it was like "chasing the wind."

Solomon concluded it was a never-ending chase because we never have enough. No matter how much we get, we always want just a little bit more. It looks enticing, but it is the way to selfishness and, ultimately, to spiritual death.

The other road has been called the hard road. This is the road of love. It is a way of life where we give ourselves up for the benefit of others and the glory of God. This road often produces short-term hardships, but in the long run, it leads us to real life.

As I mentioned earlier, I tried for many years to follow both paths. Let me assure you: it will not work. You ultimately will find yourself on one road or the other—or you will be split in two!

Following the Way of Love
I encourage you to make love your way of life. Here are some concrete suggestions:

- God is love. Let Him into your life.
- We must receive love before we can give it to others. Be thankful when others pour themselves into you.
- Be willing to spend yourself for others. Life goes sour if we don't give it away.
- Let God get the glory. It's too hot for us to handle.

It has been fashionable as we reached the year 2000 for various TV programs or magazines to try and list the most significant persons of the year, or the century, or the millennium. But I have not seen any attempt to select the most significant person in all of history.

Who do you think it would be? I think it would be Jesus. Even time is calculated from His birth. He has led millions of people for the past 2000 years. And today there are nearly 2 billion people voluntarily following Him—more than have followed any other leader in history.

Why do they follow Him? It isn't for wealth or power, is it? No, it's because they have seen in Him something that is radically different, sometimes even opposite, from the world around them. One basic difference is that He came to serve rather than to be served. And behind that mark of service is His real hallmark:

Love! Unselfish, sacrificial love that has revolutionized the world wherever it has been applied!

Not everyone accepts Jesus as God in the flesh, but no one denies His goodness or the effect for good He has had in every time and place where He has been lifted up as an example.

So if you want to know how to follow the path of love, follow Jesus. Love isn't so much a creed or a principle; it's a person. See what He says and does, and then follow Him.

Conclusion

Now we come to the end of our time together. It is my prayer that each of you will find real faith, hope, and love. And that when you look back at the end of the marriages, careers, and life work you are now beginning, you will conclude:

It has been a wonderful, magnificent journey.
Along with the joy, there have been hard times
and lots of tears,
but the rewards were more than I ever dreamed were possible.
I wouldn't have missed this trip for the world!

Blessings On You All.

From Grandpa With Love

Part III

Discipling and Mentoring

And the things you have heard me say
in the presence of many witnesses
entrust to reliable men
who will also be qualified to teach others.
(2 Timothy 2:2)

Preface

2005

As Jesus prepared to leave His disciples and return to Heaven, He passed the torch to their generation, saying, "go and make disciples..." (Matthew 28:19).

As I reached age 80 this summer, and a new great-grandchild was born, I became doubly aware that my generation is approaching the finish line, and the time for us to carry out this commission and pass the torch is coming to an end.

I decided, therefore, to place in written form some of what God has been teaching me (particularly during the last thirty six years as His disciple) about discipling and mentoring, with the prayer that it will help others who are also seeking to be His disciples. (I recognize that "discipling" is not actually a term, but I have adopted it here since it is descriptive and in somewhat common usage.)

If you have read some of my earlier writings, you may recognize familiar principles and illustrations as you go through this material. I am aware of the repetition, but it seems appropriate to reuse them here, because they are central to what I have learned about discipling and mentoring.

I'll try and give you the best I have. But remember, this is just one man's story, and we all have only part of God's message, and we also all have error. So test what I have written against the scriptures, other Godly counsel, and the leading of the Holy Spirit.

May God richly bless you, as you follow Him.

From Grandpa With Love

Discipling and Mentoring

Our family was gathered for a special family dinner to celebrate my 80th birthday. I sat with my wife Ellie and looked around with thanksgiving at our children, grandchildren, great-grandchild, and other family members whom we loved—and realized how faithfully God had multiplied and cared for us all these years. I was overwhelmed with joy!

But I was also aware of a heavy sense of responsibility that has increasingly caused me to pause and ask myself,

> "How well am I doing at passing on to others what has been shared with me about life, and particularly about our Father in Heaven, His Word, His Son Jesus, and His Spirit?"

Some people call this discipling or mentoring. But whatever you call it, I think it is vital that we receive from those who have gone before us, and that we pass on what is good to those around us, and to those who follow us. Most of what I say will be from my own experiences. Early in my law training, I learned that "hearsay" testimony from a witness was generally not admissible as evidence, since the courts usually didn't want to know what we hear others say, but rather what we ourselves have seen and heard and experienced.

Also, because of my age, I am writing from my perspective as a great-grandfather. But I have also been a child, then a parent, and later a grandparent. So as I tell you my story, sometimes I will be the learner and sometimes I will be the one who is passing on what I have learned, because that is the way it happens as we go through life.

For simplification, I will often use the masculine gender as inclusive, keeping in mind that the Bible clearly reflects that older women are to train younger women (Titus 2:4–5).

Defining Discipling and Mentoring

I think it will be helpful to clarify two terms here at the outset: disciple and mentor. Disciple is a biblical term. It refers to one who follows as a learner or pupil; it is used most often in the New Testament to refer to those who followed Jesus. By contrast, mentor does not appear in the Bible. Instead, it comes from Greek mythology and was the name of Odysseus' trusted counselor. Although the terms are somewhat intermingled today, there is a difference. In essence, I believe that one who disciples is a father and one who mentors is a grandfather. The father figure disciples us, by yoking and walking closely with us for a period of time until we are trained enough to walk alone. The grandfather is the person we go to for advice and counsel after we can walk alone, but still need occasional counsel from an older and wiser head. I believe we need both disciplers and mentors.

Recognizing Discipling and Mentoring

As I look back, I realize I have been discipled and mentored all my life, although I did not know it by those terms. First were my parents, with whom I lived the first eighteen years of my life. I am profoundly grateful for all they poured into me as they raised me to maturity. Much of what I am, and have done, came from them. And they were assisted by every teacher and authority figure that worked with me as I was growing up. Spending thirty three months in the Air Force during World War II brought me in contact with many other instructors and leaders. Then came college and Law School at Kansas University where dozens of professors and others helped to mold my life. In 1948, my wife and I were married while we were still at KU and we began our family. Here let me say that she had more impact on my life than any other person—and why not, since we were married over three times as long as I lived with my parents. I will be forever in her debt!

I encourage you never to forget how rich and deep can be the teachings we receive and give to one another in marriage, if we will only listen and learn.

Discipling By Employers
After graduating from Law School in 1951, I quickly found I was not a fully trained lawyer. I had been given a foundation of theory and knowledge, but I needed at least three to five years of practical experience and on-the-job training before I could function on my own as an attorney.

I believe we all need a time of apprenticeship as we begin a new area of work. And just as our early training by our parents deeply impacts the values and disciplines that affect our thoughts and actions throughout all our lives, so our initial bosses have great influence on the values and disciplines we will use throughout our work lives. While we cannot choose our parents, it is important that we try and choose carefully those who will train and disciple us during the early years of our careers.

My first job after Law School was in Wichita, with a sole practitioner in his 40s. Our office was in a large downtown office building, which in those days had spittoons in the hallways and elevator operators.

My boss was a business-oriented lawyer who trained me in business and probate law. But he made it clear from the beginning that he had hired me to handle any litigation we had, so I was on my own as a trial lawyer. I know I missed a great deal not having a trainer to instruct me in trial work, but it also taught me a valuable lesson: If you don't have a trainer, go find one!

For me it meant going to the courthouse and watching experienced trial lawyers at work, and joining forces with other firms when necessary. I have concluded that many of us may not have formal trainers to apprentice us in certain areas (including parents and grandparents), but there are usually substitutes around if we will look for them and ask for guidance.

Discipling By Writers

Over the next few years, my family and law practice expanded. During my 30s and early 40s I found myself continuing to search more deeply for the real meaning in life.

I expect many of you made a complete surrender to Jesus as Lord of your life at an early age. But I fought with God for many years and didn't fully surrender until I was 44 years old. During these years I met no Christian in the workplace whose lifestyle made a significant impact on me. While such persons were undoubtedly present, I was not aware of them. From my closed position, it seemed no one was able concurrently to speak out and to live out the principles of the Christian faith in real life. I saw full-time professional Christians who were expected to be holy, but for the rest of us our work worlds seemed to operate on the hard realities of life that might or might not conform with scriptural principles.

Gradually my search took me into books that I discovered had been written by others whose search paralleled my own. Later I realized that I was being discipled by these writers whom I had never met! I encourage you to use such writers to help you learn. As one older saint said to me, "You can walk with the greats. All you have to do is take them off the shelf."

For me, studying history and people's lives, especially those in the Bible, has been very helpful. These men and women have deeply impacted my life as I walked with them through scripture. It takes time and study, but it is very worthwhile. For example, tracing the Apostle Peter through the Gospels as a young man while he learned from Jesus, and then following him as a mature man as he led the early church in the Book of Acts, has totally changed how I view 1st and 2nd Peter, the two short books Peter wrote as he approached the time he was to leave this earth.

First Spiritual Discipler
Although I was receiving teaching and training in books, I was still spiritually lonely. I had family, professional, and social fellowship, but like so many men (as I would later discover), I had no other man with a kindred spirit to talk with and walk with in the difficult and eternal issues of life. Finally, in desperation, I called a man I had met briefly when he and his family visited our church one Sunday. There was something about his presence and conversation, as confirmed to me by others who knew him, that made me believe he knew something about Christian fellowship that I wanted.

Looking back now I realize the hunger that was evident in my telephone request to him. I simply announced, "I have been reading about Christian fellowship, and I would like to know where I can find some." He didn't laugh or give me the name of a church to attend, or a pastor to see, or books to read. Instead, he graciously began to meet with me on a regular basis and take me with him as he followed Christ.

The Bible says Jesus chose twelve to "be with Him" (Mark 3:14). As helpful as studies and discipleship courses are, I have concluded the best description of discipleship is to follow Jesus' example and the example I was given:

"Take someone with you as you follow Jesus."

They learn as we learn; they laugh and cry as we laugh and cry; they risk as we risk. As one man told a group of us, "We are fellows in the same ship together; only some are a little further forward than others, and they pass the information they've received back to those who follow."

I have found that whether we are taking our children with us, or having young lawyers side by side with us, or spending time with a spiritual child in the faith, the principle Jesus called yoking is a key ingredient. As Jesus said:

take my yoke upon you and learn from me...
(Matthew 11:29a)

For the next three or four years my friend and I spent much time yoked together as we studied, memorized scripture, prayed, and shared our faith in familiar and unfamiliar places. I can never adequately express my gratitude. It is a key reason that I have tried to pass on these same lessons to those who were following me.

I have concluded that we need earthly parents to train us to think and act rightly in our early life, good bosses to train us competently and ethically in the early stages of our work life, and spiritual fathers to walk with us and help us to mature as we begin our life with Christ. As Paul wrote to the Corinthians:

> *Even though you have ten thousand guardians in Christ,*
> *you do not have many fathers,*
> *for in Christ Jesus I became your father through the gospel.*
> *Therefore, I urge you to imitate me.*
> (I Corinthians 4:15–16)

It is a rare privilege when God gives us such a person to guide and train us. And it is also a deep responsibility when God gives us a physical child, a working apprentice, or a spiritual child to walk with us and imitate us. For that reason, it is important that we also learn, both for ourselves and for those who follow us, to heed carefully Paul's additional and sober warning:

> *Follow my example,* ***as I follow the example of Christ.***
> (I Corinthians 11:1, emphasis added)

Remember, we are helping others become disciples of Christ, not disciples or clones of ourselves.

First Spiritual Mentor

I met my first spiritual mentor in the same way I obtained my first spiritual discipler. By asking! The New Testament writer, James, admonishes us:

> *You do not have, because you do not ask God.*
> (James 4:2b)

I have determined that those of us who want to receive all God has for us must humble ourselves and become spiritual beggars. We must cast all our pride and false egoism aside and ask Him and His servants for help!

Since my own father died when I was 26 years old, and I knew no older spiritual grandfather figure locally, I decided to call three writers whose books had helped me in my quest. Two of them were so busy we couldn't make contact. However, my call to Dr. Elton Trueblood changed my life. A biography of him was subtitled *Believer, Teacher, Friend.* And he was.

At that time he was probably in his 70s and a professor, as well as a Pastor, at a small Christian college. Although I was totally unknown to him, he welcomed my call and invited me to come for a visit. On the day I arrived, he had prepared a guest room for me. Then he spent the entire next day answering my questions and helping me sort out the direction my life should now take. I'll never forget his opening comment that was so unusual in our hurried, harried world. He smiled and said, "We have time! Isn't that wonderful? We have time!"

Mentors, like grandfathers, have time, and they are willing to share it with those who ask. Be careful to seek mentors and disciplers who have time, and be aware that you will need to take time if you want to disciple or mentor others.

A constant theme I received from all those who discipled, mentored, and taught me was the value of small-group relationships. I found these to be the essence of the church. Large gatherings are exciting and allow us to learn and worship, but it is only in small, more intimate settings (usually about 2 to 12 people) that we usually experience deep fellowship. Best of all, of course, is when we can talk and walk with our wives and physical families as brothers and sisters in the family of Christ.

I was also repeatedly encouraged to have a more mature Christian, a Christian peer, and a less mature Christian in my life. I think that, too, is good advice.

Being a Spiritual Discipler or Mentor

As I moved into my 50s, I was challenged one day by a man who had been investing his life in me. He said rather pointedly, "I think it is time for you to start investing your life in other people." My answer was honest but not very spiritual. I responded, "I don't think much of the idea, but because you have asked me, I will!"

I didn't realize it then, but it was to be one of the major decisions of my life. It helped me consciously change from concentrating on the temporary things of this world to becoming a stepping-stone into the amazing wonder of helping build people—who will be around for all eternity.

Since that time, my life has been enriched by so many other lives. It gives me inexpressible joy to think back on the years of walking with other searchers, sometimes to learn, sometimes to teach. Sometimes one on one, sometimes with two or more. Sometimes in a church, sometimes at home. Sometimes at a conference, or in a restaurant or workplace. Sometimes in our hometown, and sometimes in other cities or even another country. But always with people, God, and His Word.

God has given us roles in the various institutions (Family, Church, Workplace, and Government) in which he has placed us. And we have the opportunity to represent Him in every one of these areas—if we are willing. This includes not only studying and applying scriptural principles ourselves but also discipling and mentoring others. Jesus didn't hold discipleship classes. Instead, he taught and explained as he walked along day after day with those who were following him. While we can learn some principles in books, classes, and conferences that are helpful, true discipleship and mentoring will best occur in our natural settings at home, at work, in church, and in our community, modeling the life of Christ in us and then investing our lives in others who want to do the same.

Discipling and mentoring is an expected outgrowth of being bound together as parent and child, employer and employee, or leader and follower in the church or other institutions. In other instances, where no institutional relationship exists, we must decide for ourselves whether or not to start this process. In these latter cases, it seems best if the relationship begins primarily because the pupil is searching for God, not because the discipler/mentor is searching for pupils. Usually the pupil will initiate the request, but occasionally we see rare birds seriously searching, and we realize that we need to help them get started. As one friend encouraged me as we worked together, "Always keep your rare bird net ready."

If you decide to be involved in this process, here are some issues for prayer and Godly counsel that you may want to consider before you begin:

1. If you are looking for someone to disciple or mentor you:
   - Check the fruit around the tree and decide if this is the right person.
   - If so, humble yourself and ask for help.
   - Make yourself available to fit his schedule.
   - Be teachable.

2. If you are asked to disciple or mentor someone, ask yourself:
   - Is he searching and teachable?
   - Do I have what he needs, or shall I send him to someone else?
   - Am I able and willing to spend the time and energy needed?

Discipling and Mentoring in Our Older Years

Because I was older before I submitted my life to Christ, other discoveries came late as well. For example, I was in my 60s before I became consciously aware that we can be mentored by unexpected encounters with people who are not formal teachers or trainers. For me it happened one night while we were attending a dinner party given by some friends. During the evening, the hostess' mother (who was a generation older) drew me aside to talk. Since the woman and her husband were in their 80s and had been married over 60 years, I respected their experience and wisdom, so I listened attentively. She said to me, "There are two questions you'll have to ask yourself in life, Marvin. The first is 'What is your definition of success?' The second is 'How much is enough?'"

Since that time, I have found that I need to answer both of these as early as possible if I am to be and do all God has planned for me.

I encourage you to watch for these impromptu mentors who appear in your life with messages you don't want to miss. They can come unexpectedly in a sermon, a speech, or a casual conversation, but they can deeply affect our life journey.

I don't know how God will use you, but I believe He has a unique plan for all the days of our lives, including our older years. Part of that plan may include time late in life when we can continue to pass on to others what He has taught us over the years. Psalm 71:18 says it this way:

> *Even when I am old and gray, do not forsake me, O God,*
> *till I declare your power to the next generation,*
> *your might to all who are to come.*

I found each of us has our own unique part to play in God's plan, and we usually need to use the method that comes naturally for us. One particular urge for me was to bridge the gap that I saw between God's teachings and the way that I, and others, were living our everyday lives. This became a goal, never fully reached, but at least a goal.

Since I was a word person, and had been discipled by writers, I suppose it was only natural that I would begin to pass on what I was learning in the same way. As the years rolled by I began to reduce to writing many of the subjects I had been studying and attempting to apply during the previous years. Often these were then placed in small inexpensive booklets, so they could be easily read and distributed.

One booklet that I felt was particularly appropriate for our grandchildren, I placed in our lockbox with a personal note for delivery to each one as they reached age 21. Later, as our 4th generation began to arrive, my wife and I added a personal letter for each new great-grandchild—including those who might be born after we were gone.

We also claimed the following family verse:

"As for me, this is my covenant with them," says the Lord.
"My Spirit, who is on you,
and my words that I have put in your mouth
will not depart from your mouth,
or from the mouths of your children,
or from the mouths of their descendants
from this time on and forever," says the Lord.
(Isaiah 59:21)

Moses, in his final song at the end of Deuteronomy, concluded:

> *Remember the days of old;*
> *consider the generations long past.*
> *Ask your father and he will tell you,*
> *your elders, and they will explain to you.*
> (Deuteronomy, 32:7)

As I approached my 70th birthday, I decided it was time for me to visit again with someone who had already lived through some of the years up ahead. I called a man I respected who was about ten years my senior and said, "I would like to come down and talk with you about the 70s."

He agreed and we set the date.

I asked one of our teenage grandsons to go along, for the fellowship and also for what he might learn. I said, "Come on and you can learn what you need to know for your 70s." I had to smile at his honest reply: "But, Grandpa, I don't think I'll remember!"

However, he agreed to go anyway. We flew down to our host's city and met with him for about 2 or 3 hours. Here's what we heard:

First: Learn to manage deterioration. All our lives have been spent managing growth in our families, our finances, our businesses, our churches, and other institutions. It has been exciting to expand. Now we must learn the difficult art of contraction.

Second: Concentrate on the core items of life: Health, Wealth, Relationships, and Usefulness. These often interact. For example, a breakdown in relationships may cause a problem with our health. But we don't need unlimited amounts of any of these four items, only enough to be and do what God has planned for this season of our life.

Third: I then asked if there were any surprises, anything he hadn't expected when he entered this decade of life. He thought for a moment and then answered slowly, "Yes. It was much harder than I expected!"

During the intervening years, I have continued to talk with other older men and women. Some were reluctant, some felt inadequate, but all have been helpful. Recently, my wife and I moved to a retirement community. Before we moved, I had noticed that I was usually one of the oldest in many of our groups, and there seemed to be less and less opportunity to be with older folks. Now I was back being one of the younger men. And what a feast God gave me as I began to watch, listen, and learn from scores of people who have lived through many years of their '80s and '90s that I expect to encounter in the future. Hopefully, He will someday give me the opportunity to pass on what I learn.

A Final Word

Now it is time for us to close our time together. I deeply appreciate this opportunity to write to you what is in my heart. It has been a rewarding experience for me to look back over a lifetime and think about so many people who have invested their lives in me, as well as those with whom God has used me. And it is exciting to look ahead and think about the opportunities that God may give to continue learning and then passing on what we learn, until He calls us home.

In essence, discipling and mentoring are a lifestyle and not a list of rules. But this lifestyle is foundational to passing on our faith not only with our physical children and grandchildren, but also with the spiritual children and grandchildren that God may give us along the way.

If we are wise, we will learn not only from those who are above us but also from those who are beside us and behind us. If we are obedient, we will pass on these same lessons whenever, wherever, and to whomever God instructs us to do so. But always we will do it for the glory of God and for the benefit of others, and not to enhance ourselves.

Thanks for spending this time with me. I pray God will continue to bless each of you, and others through you, as you continue to receive and then pass on His love and the life messages He gives to you.

From Grandpa With Love

Part IV

Letters From Grandpa

These commandments that I give you today are to be upon your hearts.
Impress them on your children. Talk about them when you sit at home
and when you walk along the road, when you lie down
and when you get up.
Tie them as symbols on your hands and bind them on your forehead.
Write them on the doorframes of your houses and on your gates.
(Deuteronomy 6:6–9)

Preface

2007–2011

During recent years I have written "Letters From Grandpa" to our family and friends relating Biblical concepts to our lives. Some of these were occasioned by special days or times of the year, some were about current events or circumstances, and still others related to matters about which I was puzzled and finally reached a conclusion that I thought might be helpful to others.

Some of these thoughts have been germinating in my mind and life for many years. Others have appeared over the years in various writings. And certain ones have been occasioned by more recent events. But all seemed important enough to send to our family and friends.

I pray they will give you some new thoughts and encouragement for your own life.

From Grandpa With Love

Letter #1

The First Three Questions

Many people read the Bible through each year, sometimes using various versions for new insights and understanding. I have found it a profitable discipline that takes about twenty minutes a day. As I begin to read each year, I am struck by the way the first few chapters set the stage for the rest of the Book—and particularly how three early questions reveal a theme of three major issues that are encountered by every generation.

Genesis 1 and 2 describe God's creation of the world and the beginning of life as God places mankind in a perfect world, called the Garden of Eden. Genesis 3 and 4 set forth three events that occur in every life:

- We are tempted and disobey God;
- We are ashamed, hide from God, and called to confess;
- We are alienated from God and other people, and destined for eternal death when our natural lives are over, unless we confess, surrender our will to God, and accept responsibility to help our brothers.

Let's call these Temptation, Confession, and Action. The events are framed by three questions:

- The First Question Satan asks Man.
- The First Question God asks Man.
- The First Question Man asks God.

Every individual, in every generation, must face these same three questions.

Temptation

"Did God really say...?"
(Genesis 3:1)

(The First Question Satan Asks Man)

Temptation can be defined as "enticement to sin, to do wrong." Satan originally tempted Eve by enticing her to question God's command given to Adam before her creation:

> *...you must not eat from the tree*
> *of the knowledge of good and evil,*
> *for when you eat of it you will surely die*
> (Genesis 2:17)

Satan slyly tempts Eve by asking, "Did God really say...?" to question both the truth of God's command and Adam's reliability as he repeats it. Satan then tells Eve she will not die and that she can "be like God, knowing good and evil" (Genesis 3:4–5). This is the same boast made by Satan that cast him "down to the grave, to the depths of the pit." (Isaiah 14:15). As Eve and then Adam succumb, they join Satan's dark world.

The same temptation is used today to entice us to disobey God, as we are asked by skeptics, "Did God really say...?" If God's Word can be made to seem unreliable, whether by ridicule, logic, or majority rule, there is no reason to obey Him. This then allows us to accept Satan's delusion that we ourselves can "be like God, knowing good and evil."

But, if we are in daily communion with God, His Word and His people, our faith is strengthened, and we know better how and what to answer when we are tempted by someone asking,

"Did God really say…?"

Confession

"Where are you?"
(Genesis 3:9)

(The First Question God Asks Man)

When Adam disobeyed God's command by eating the forbidden fruit, he was afraid and hid from God (Genesis 3:1–10). Instead of confessing that he had eaten the fruit, he compounded his problem by blaming both God and Eve!

> *The man said, "The woman **you** put here with me—*
> ***she** gave me some fruit from the tree, and I ate it."*
> (Genesis 3:12, emphasis supplied)

Disobedience is common to us all (Romans 3:23). And the consequence of our disobedience is always the same. It separates us from our Creator, until we stop hiding, confess (agree) that we have disobeyed, and repent by turning around and start walking back to God. Somewhere in my life, I finally realized that I always need to walk in the presence of God, no matter where it may lead and even though the road ahead seems difficult. It's just too hard, and too deadly, to walk alone!

Now when we hear God ask, **"Where are you?"** I pray we will remember John's advice:

> *If we claim to be without sin, we deceive ourselves*
> *and the truth is not in us.*
> *If we confess our sins, he is faithful and just*
> *and will forgive us our sins and purify us from all unrighteousness.*
> (1 John 1:8–9)

Action

"Am I my brother's keeper?"
(Genesis 4:9b)

(The First Question Man Asks God)

When Adam disobeyed God by eating the forbidden fruit, and then "hid from the Lord" rather than confessing and walking with God, "the Lord God banished him from the Garden of Eden…" (Genesis 3:23–24). From that time on, mankind has sinned in every generation and reaped natural death as a result. But God quickly revealed He also offers us a remedy.

After leaving the Garden, Adam and Eve had two sons, Cain and Abel. When these boys were grown, Abel pleased God with his actions, but Cain did not. Cain became angry and downcast. God warned:

> *If you do what is right, will you not be accepted?*
> *But if you do not do what is right,*
> *sin is crouching at your door;*
> *it desires to have you, but you must master it.*
> (Genesis 4:7)

Regrettably, sin won the battle. Cain invited his brother, Abel, out to a field and killed him. When God called Cain to account, he responded with mankind's first question that has echoed through every generation:

Am I my brother's keeper?

The answer seems to be a simple:

Yes!

From Grandpa With Love

Letter #2

What Must I Do To Inherit Eternal Life?

Each spring we celebrate Easter and the Resurrection of Jesus. As we do, it reminds us that natural life is God's gift to us all, and eternal life is God's great gift to those who become part of His family.

Enclosed are some thoughts that have helped me and I pray will be helpful to you.

Balancing Our Love For God and For People

The Bible is centered on two basic relationships: God and people—and we are to love them both (Leviticus 19:18; Deuteronomy 6:5; Luke 10:27). It might be called the "pathway of the cross," stretching vertically up to God and horizontally out to our fellow man—an easy maxim to state, but a difficult one to keep in balance. As a result, many of us major in one and minor in the other.

For me, an excellent illustration of this dual dilemma is found by reading Luke 10 and 18 as two parts of the same balancing act. These two scriptures recount Jesus' conversations with two men who came to Him, each asking the identical question:

What must I do to inherit eternal life?

One majored in God; the other majored in people. As a result they each needed, and each received, a different answer—but

94

each answer was only part of the whole and was apparently given to offset the imbalance in each man's one-sided view.

The Good Samaritan (Luke 10:25–37)

The first inquirer was described as "an expert in the law." As such, he was akin to the "priest" and the "Levite" described in the story Jesus used to answer the lawyer's question, since all three men were set apart for the religious duties of Jewish life. As a religious man, the lawyer already knew the Biblical answer to his own question, i.e., "love God" and "love your neighbor."

But, like the priest and the Levite in Jesus' story, he hesitated to reach out horizontally toward *all* people. Apparently all their religious eyes were so fixed upward toward God that they couldn't see any need to assist or to be involved with people like the wounded stranger left by robbers on the side of the road. The expert lawyer had a narrow, unbalanced view of his "neighbor," so Jesus opened his eyes through a compassionate Samaritan's aid to a stricken stranger, whom the holy men wouldn't help!

The Rich Young Ruler (Luke 18:18–30)

The second inquirer was a man who had kept, from boyhood, five of the horizontal (people) parts of the Ten Commandments: those relating to adultery, murder, stealing, false testimony, and honoring parents. But when Jesus told him to "sell everything you have and give to the poor" and "come, follow me," i.e., get right vertically with God, he couldn't do it.

His eyes were apparently so fixed outward toward people that he never looked upward toward God, who had given him all the wealth he had been distributing as his own gift. In effect, his money was his god, and he couldn't let go!

Different Answers for Different Blindness

Wealth apparently didn't enter into the first man's problem. Instead, he was simply blind to the personal needs of people he met in his everyday life. As someone has said, "He was so heavenly minded that he was no earthly good." He wasn't hooked on money, but he forgot that his purpose in life was not simply personal piety and purity but also to help others. Jesus answered this lawyer by showing him he needed to open his eyes horizontally to see and to help any people that God put in his path. Hopefully, he obeyed.

The second man's problem did involve wealth, because it blinded him from seeing and following God. When the rich young man was told where to give his money, and to do it all at one time, he declined. Obeying Jesus would have freed him from this competing god. Sadly, he refused—but who knows, perhaps he, too, ultimately surrendered.

Like all Jesus' stories, these two probably have multiple meanings and interpretations. We each hear the stories from our own backgrounds and circumstances, and thus see different applications. I have found it is wise, therefore, to listen to interpreters from many backgrounds. And also to combine the teachings in one scripture with teachings in other scriptures so we can maintain a balanced view of life.

A Family Issue

This brings me, as a retired lawyer, to one more question: Why did each inquirer ask what he must "do" to "inherit," when, in fact, inheritance is not based on what we do, but on our *relationship* with the donor? Could it be that both men (as well as most of us who hear these stories) intuitively realize the need to become part of the Family of God if we want to "inherit" eternal life from our Father?

The Apostle John made it clear we become God's children by receiving and believing in Jesus:

> *Yet to all who received him, to those who believed in his name,*
> *he gave the right to become children of God—*
> *children born not of natural descent,*
> *nor of human decision or a husband's will, but born of God.*
> (John 1:12–13)

When we are born again (as Jesus discusses in John 3) and become part of the Family of God, we have standing to "inherit" our Father's priceless gift of eternal life. And it is only when we become "children of God" that we seem able and willing to carry out His dual command:

> *"Love the Lord your God with all your heart and with all your soul*
> *and with all your strength and with all your mind,"*
> *and*
> *"Love your neighbor as yourself."*
> (Luke 10:27)

Letter #3

Why Do I Call Him Jesus?

When Grandma and I first began dating, I had to decide, "What do I call her parents?" At first it was "Mr." and "Mrs.," but over the years it changed to "Church" for her father and "Mom" for her mother. We refer (and relate) to people differently, based upon the intimacy of our relationship.

A Person Named Jesus

The Gospels record that those who knew the Son of God personally used His personal name, Jesus. It is recorded over *1200 times* in the Bible. It was the name "Jesus" that the Apostles were ordered by the authorities not to use (Acts 4:18), and it is the name that seems to be the hardest to use or to carry today. Somehow we feel almost sacrilegious when we think of addressing God intimately as we would a friend.

An Officeholder

Jesus was also known by the office he came to fulfill, that of "the Christ" (i.e., the one God had anointed to save us and ultimately to rule His Kingdom). Early followers who didn't walk with him in the flesh (such as the Apostle Paul) often said "Christ" or "Christ Jesus" or "Jesus Christ" when they spoke of Him. The Bible uses the term "Christ" about *500 times.*

Somehow it still seems easier, and perhaps more respectful, to talk about His office, i.e., the "Christ" or "Christ Jesus," than it is to address this person whom we have never seen by His given name. Yet it was this simple name, Jesus, that our Lord used to identify Himself when Paul was struck blind on the road to Damascus (Acts 9:5)!

The Head of a Group

Finally, Jesus is sometimes known as the founder of a religion or organization that we call Christianity. When we are asked to identify our faith, we are often given choices such as Jew, Christian, or Muslim. While "Christian" is a common term today, it appears only three times in the Bible! Instead, the early followers of Jesus often referred to each other by their intimate personal relationship as a "brother" or "sister" (Acts 9:17; Romans 16:1). They didn't see themselves as members of a religion or an organization, but as a family of persons who were becoming one with each other and with Jesus, whom they had come to know and to love personally (John 17; Ephesians 4).

A Question and An Answer

So how do we have a personal relationship with Jesus? How do we get on a first-name basis? How do we become comfortable speaking to Jesus, or about Jesus, (rather than thinking of Him as a high officeholder or ourselves as members of a religious organization) so we can have a personal relationship with this Person whom we seek to follow?

Let me tell you some of the things that have helped me. Perhaps they will also be meaningful for you.

First, I Had To Surrender

I finally faced the question we all face: "Shall I accept Jesus as God?" It hadn't seemed possible for a person to be man and God. But, when I finally surrendered and accepted Him as divine as a matter of faith, and gave God all my life I was able to give, it all began to make some sense (John 1:11–14; Colossians 2:9; 1 John 2:22–23, 4:2, 15). The Bible says we are to "become like little children" (Matthew 18:3). When we do, we have no problem seeing Jesus personally. It's easy for children to talk to Jesus or to sing "Jesus loves me, this I know."

Next, I Had To Stay Close to God
Some time ago I asked one of our daughters, "How do you know if someone loves you?" Her answer was very simple, but profound. "If they want to be with you." I decided if I really loved Jesus, I would want to spend time with Him. And the more time we spent together, the closer we became. If I disobeyed, our personal relationship became broken until I confessed and straightened things out.

Finally, I Found I Had To Stay Close To Other People
Jesus said we were to love others as He loved us (John 13:34). That was hard for me. But He was right. And it has to be individuals—not just people as a whole. As one man said, "I love the world; it's the guy next door I can't stand!" I found I needed personal relationships with other individuals if I was going to have a personal relationship with Jesus. This required that I spend time with them. It also required that I learn to forgive others, and work at keeping my relationships with them, if I wanted God to forgive me and get our personal relationship back together when I got off the track (Matthew 6:12–15; Ephesians 4:32).

It's been forty years since I first surrendered and started walking with Jesus. It has gotten sweeter every day. I praise God that I am called a Christian. I revere the One we call the Christ. But I feel much closer to Him when we stay on a first-name basis, and I can simply and lovingly call Him:

Jesus!

I hope that will also be true for you!

From Grandpa With Love

Letter #4

Why Do We Do What We Do?

Someone once challenged me, "Why we do something may be the most important question we ask ourselves." In other words, "What is our motivation?"

Simply stated, I believe we are motivated by gain or loss, as these relate both to the future and to the past. Since this is such a fundamental, yet subtle, issue in life, I have spent many years trying first, to understand the concept, and then to apply it in my own life. I hope it will be helpful for you.

The Bible says,

> *Test everything. Hold on to the good.*
> *Avoid every kind of evil.*
> (1 Thessalonians 5:21–22)

So, as usual, I encourage you to hold on to that which is good (of God)—and discard the rest.

Seeking Rewards (Gain or Loss in the Future)

Looking forward, we seem to act out of hope of gain or fear of loss. Thus, in spiritual terms, many are motivated by the thought of spending their future in either Heaven or Hell. In the stock market arena, analysts note that many investors are motivated to buy, sell, or hold because of fear or greed. In politics, voters often cast their ballots for the candidates they believe will help them the most and/or hurt them the least.

In other words we seek to be rewarded in the future for our efforts by getting what we want and by avoiding what we don't want. We want money, but no debt. We want recognition, but no shame. We want health, but no sickness. The list is virtually endless, but it usually seems tied to a desire to be rewarded by receiving some kind of gain and/or avoiding some kind of loss.

Such motivation for rewards is powerful, but it can also be selfish and destructive. As soon as I act in order to obtain the reward, I am in danger of living by my works rather than by God's grace (Ephesians 2:8–9). This can make me or my group the focal point; bring pride when I do well and despair when I fail; make me the giver and result in arrogance; cause me to expect a reward for what I have accomplished; give me a false sense of self-esteem because of what I have done, which can disappear if I fail to do well; and cause me to lose a major reason for living when I can no longer perform.

Receiving An Inheritance (Gain or Loss in the Past)

While anticipation of future rewards is an important motivator and discussed often in the Bible, I do not believe it is as powerful as the motivation we can receive by looking back—in other words, by gratitude or revenge because of what has occurred in the past.

Since revenge is not allowed for Christians (Romans 12:19), I have concluded that I want to do what I do because of gratitude for what God has done, or will do, for me. Thus, I do not strive and work here on earth in order to get a better place in Heaven. Instead, I try (not always successfully) to do what I do out of gratitude for God giving me life, and loving me and saving me for eternal life—and because I want Him to be glorified, and pleased with what I am and do.

The basic issue is not what I do for God, but what God does for and through me!

When my motivation comes from gratitude for God's grace rather than my effort to get a reward, it makes God and others the focal point of my life; brings humility instead of pride; and makes me want to give thanks for receiving what I didn't earn, instead of claiming a reward for my efforts. Since my self-worth comes because God loves me as His child, I never lose my self-esteem whether or not I perform well in this world; and my reason for living continues as long as God has me living, since He can use me as a receiver even when I can no longer be a giver.

In both cases we work and strive for excellence, but one is for my glory or advantage, while the other is to glorify God and help others. Like the movie *Chariots of Fire*, in which one man ran for the Olympic medal and the other because he felt God's pleasure when he ran.

We receive a reward because of what we do (*Works of man*). We receive an inheritance because of whose we are (*Grace of God*). While there is much discussion and debate about receiving Heavenly rewards for what we do on earth, there is an interesting verse in Colossians 3:23–24:

> *Whatever you do, work at it with all your heart,*
> *as working for the Lord, not for men,*
> *since you know that you will **receive an inheritance***
> ***from the Lord as a reward.***
> (Emphasis supplied.)

Doesn't it seem possible that being with God for eternity is, in itself, both our inheritance and our reward?

I have wondered if the story of the Prodigal Son and his Father and Older Brother did not include this point. You may recall that when the Prodigal Son came home his Father was joyful and welcomed him with open arms and a great feast. The Older Brother was angry and complained to his Father:

"Look! All these years I've been slaving for you and never disobeyed your orders. Yet you never gave me even a young goat so I could celebrate with my friends. But when this son of yours who has squandered your property with prostitutes comes home, you kill the fattened calf for him!"
"My son," the father said,
"you are always with me and everything I have is yours.
But we had to celebrate and be glad,
because this brother of yours was dead and is alive again;
he was lost and is found."
(Luke 15:29–32, emphasis added)

Each of us must decide:

Do I work in order to receive a future reward from God,
-or do I work because of gratitude-
trusting Him as my Father to provide for me,
now and forever?

The work may be the same, but the effect on me
and those around me may be vastly different!

From Grandpa With Love

Letter #5

How Can We Get It Right?

Some time ago a man who believed in reincarnation said to me, "I think we keep coming back after death until we get it right." I asked him, "Who do you know that got it right?" He looked puzzled and, after thinking about my question for a moment, said very quietly, "No one!"

I believe the man's desire was good, but his solution was wrong. Each year we celebrate Easter to proclaim again that God is the only One Who can get it right! Below are some concepts that have helped me understand why we all need Jesus. I pray they will also aid you.

The Struggle

It is hard to think of anything much worse than being recalled to this life again and again throughout all eternity, futilely attempting to get it right.

While few in our society believe any one individual has ever, or can ever, get it right, many of us (including myself at one time) do seem to believe that our human race, in the aggregate, will get it right if we just keep on trying long enough. It is a little like the man who said he lost money on each item he sold but insisted that everything would work out right, if he could just make enough sales!

We strive, generation after generation, century after century, millennium after millennium, to get it right by ourselves. And always, we fail. When we solve one problem, another arises to take its place. New political leaders soon wear out and become the entrenched machine we want to eliminate. Diseases are conquered so we can live longer, only to discover the proliferation of new age problems that engulf our society. We solve the imbalance in our economic system by creating ever-larger corporate masters and huge governments, only to find the economy of scale has given way to bloated, bureaucratic inefficiency. Governments, companies, and individuals temporarily improve their lifestyles by borrowing ever-increasing amounts of money, only to end in economic disaster. Welfare systems meant to help needy children, mothers, and other vulnerable people in society often destroy families and produce unloved children and inner-city wastelands. The list of these mutations is virtually endless.

While we have made great strides in science, economics, and politics, our human nature has never improved. The problem is not in society; it is in mankind. We have a fatal flaw that won't go away. We do what we shouldn't, and we don't do what we should. When we get into groups, we magnify rather than eliminate our dilemma.

Young people are idealistic and believe they can make the world better. They can and do make improvements, but they can never change the nature of the people. Thus, each generation strives, but ultimately fails, to get it right during its lifetime.

I belong to the generation born before the Great Depression of the 1930s; we became the victors in World War II. Since we have been nicknamed the "Greatest Generation," if any group in history would get it right, surely it would be us.

But, as we come to the end of our generation, I, like old men of every generation, woefully conclude that it didn't happen in my lifetime. As we prepare to complete our life journey, the world still has the same recurring evils of war, poverty, disease, crime, and abuse—and for the first time, total annihilation of the whole world may now be possible with biological and nuclear weapons of mass destruction.

At the close of World War II, General Douglas McArthur addressed the world with these words:

> "We have had our last chance. If we do not now devise some greater and more equitable system, Armageddon will be at our door. The problem basically is theological and involves a spiritual recrudescence and improvement of human character that will synchronize with our almost matchless advances in science, art, literature, and all material and cultural developments of the past 2000 years. It must be of the spirit if we are to save the flesh."

Mankind has been trying to change human nature by our own efforts since Cain killed Abel at the dawn of history. We haven't succeeded. We will never succeed, because the human race didn't create itself and it cannot perfect itself. Human pride says we can. History and human nature says we can't. We can't because we aren't God. We are not the Creator; we are the created. We need something more than our own human abilities if we are ever going to get it right.

The Answer

The answer to our dilemma seems difficult for strong-willed people to accept, but it is actually rather simple if we are willing to receive it: *Stop trying to change our old nature by our own efforts—then humble ourselves and let God exchange our old faulty human nature for a new nature through Christ!*

The Bible explains it this way:

> *So I say, live by the spirit, and you will not gratify the desires*
> *of the sinful nature. For the sinful nature desires*
> *what is contrary to the Spirit,*
> *and the Spirit what is contrary to the sinful nature.*
> *They are in conflict with each other,*
> *so that you do not do what you want...*
> *The acts of the sinful nature are obvious:*
> *sexual immorality, impurity, and debauchery;*
> *idolatry and witchcraft; hatred, discord, jealousy, fits of rage,*
> *selfish ambition, dissensions, factions, and envy;*
> *drunkenness, orgies and the like.*
> *I warn you, as I did before, that those who live like this will not inherit*
> *the kingdom of God.*
> *But the fruit of the Spirit is love, joy, peace, patience, kindness,*
> *goodness, faithfulness, gentleness and self control...*
> *Those who belong to Christ Jesus*
> *have crucified the sinful nature with its passions and desires.*
> (Galatians 5:16–17, 19–24)

Thank God. He has shown us how to "get it right." All we have to do is accept Jesus. As we surrender, God is glorified, and He can use us to reveal a dim glimpse into the perfect Kingdom He will bring when Jesus comes again. Until then, we celebrate His sacrifice for us, work for good—and echo,

Come, Lord Jesus!

From Grandpa With Love

Letter #6

Unity or Uniformity?

I pray also...that all of them may be one...
May they be brought to complete unity...
(John 17:20–23)

As Jesus prepared to leave the earth, He prayed that His followers would be one, not in outward appearance but as diverse, living parts of Christ's Body. The Bible calls this "unity." By contrast, worldly organizations and institutions often seek to create one-ness by having their members dress alike, talk alike, act alike, and even think alike. This may look like oneness on the outside, but in reality it is simply oneness in form, held together by force. We call this "uniformity."

While some form is necessary, the term uniformity never appears in the Bible!

About thirty years ago, I traveled to Colorado Springs with a man who was kind enough to take me with him for a Leighton Ford Evangelistic Reach-Out. It marked my life for good in many ways. Of particular importance was our conversation on the road about Jesus' prayer for His followers in John 17, some of whom had traveled with Him for three years—and most importantly, as it related to the subject of oneness with one another and with Him.

I have pondered and thought about this for many years. I have become increasingly concerned that we can so easily shift our focus and incorporate a worldly view about the subject. So I decided to share some comparisons that God has laid on my heart.

Unity emphasizes the *individual*;
Uniformity emphasizes the *institution*.

Unity puts *freedom* first;
Uniformity puts *order* first.

Unity comes because we *want to obey*;
Uniformity comes because we *have to obey*.

Unity requires *internal discipline*;
Uniformity requires *external discipline*.

Unity has an *invisible, Heavenly King*;
Uniformity has *visible, worldly kings*.

Unity is a *rainbow*;
Uniformity is *one color*.

Unity is *harmony*;
Uniformity is *one note*.

Unity is recognized by a *radiant countenance*;
Uniformity is recognized by a *man-made uniform*.

Unity is a *warm body*;
Uniformity is a *cold machine*.

Unity spreads through *relationships*;
Uniformity suppresses through *rules*.

Unity is based on *love*;
Uniformity is based on *law*.

*How good and pleasant it is
when brothers live together in unity!*
(Psalm 133:1)

*Make every effort to keep the unity of the Spirit
through the bond of peace.*
(Ephesians 4:3)

From Grandpa With Love

Letter #7

Getting and Giving

There is a great emphasis today, in both Christian and secular circles, on material wealth. As a result, it is tempting to fall into the Old Testament approach that often equated wealth with goodness.

As one young man asked recently, "How come all these books are written by rich men?" To which his companion replied, "Because no one would read them if they weren't!"

Because the subject of money and wealth is so broad and discussed so much in the Bible as well as today, it seems good to send you some personal thoughts on "Getting and Giving." Again, these are from my perspective, so hold on to what is good (of God)—and discard the rest.

Be creators, not exploiters. Learn to get as God wants before we try to give as He wants.

Don't embezzle. God created it all and owns it all, so never claim everything as ours.

Don't boast. Worldly wealth is an outgrowth of the gifts God has given us, so give Him the credit.

Ask God where He wants it to go. Think of ourselves as distributors of God's possessions, rather than givers of what we own.

Live simply. How much we give is often not as important (nor as difficult) as how much we try and keep for me and mine.

Build people, not fortunes. Consider distributing our gifts and talents to help those traveling with us so they can also become effective distributors, instead of simply accumulating worldly wealth ourselves so we can become big givers.

Seek to be productive, not just profitable. Profitability and growth will follow if we follow Biblical principles and God so desires.

Finish what God gives us to do. Whatever God entrusts to us, consider distributing ourselves, rather than transferring it to others to distribute.

Don't miss the joy of scattering as we go through life. Distribute what we are given during our lifetime. Those who accumulate and give at death are simply giving away what they couldn't keep anyway.

Don't try to rule from the grave. Accept the principle of the "rule against perpetuities." Future generations may rue the day we set up corporations and foundations for perpetuity. These take on a life of their own, and they may not do what we planned; in fact, those in control after we die may use this wealth to fight against what we believed and were trying to accomplish.

Put God and His Word and His Spirit, not worldly wealth, at our center. Everything we are and do will flow from our core. It is much more important to give others our faith than our money.

Attached is a poem I wrote several years ago that seems appropriate for our discussion. I hope it all helps.

From Grandpa With Love

Wealth and Worry

If you've got it, don't hoard it, don't bury it in the ground.
If you've got it, then share it, begin to spread it around.

If your eyes light up, when your bank account grows,
It's dark inside of you, everybody knows;
So serve your King, from your head to your toes,
Then your treasure in heaven will grow.

Don't worry about your living, what you'll eat, drink or wear.
Don't worry about your body, don't you know God cares?
If He cares for all the flowers, and the little birds, too;
Surely you can believe Him, that He cares about you!

Don't worry about tomorrow, afraid of what it will bring.
Just seek your Lord and His righteousness,
He'll make your heart sing!

Let your eyes light up, from your deeds, not your dough;
Let His light inside of you, start to show.
As you serve your King, you'll begin to glow.
You'll be rich in Heaven, I know!
You'll be rich in Heaven, I know!

Letter #8

What About The Lottery?

Casting the lot settles disputes
and keeps strong opponents apart.
(Proverbs 18:18)

Our local community recently voted against having a state casino located here. Because Kansas has reversed from prohibiting to promoting the Lottery and other forms of gambling in recent years, I thought it might be helpful to look at the origin and early use of the "lot" as a valid method of reconciliation and deciding disputes—and see how easy it is to turn one of God's useful gifts into a way to pander to a lower desire to get something for nothing.

Again, these are from my perspective, so hold on to what is good (of God)—and discard the rest.

Lot

Approximately 4000 years ago, Abram (later known as the patriarch, Abraham) and his nephew, Lot, both dwelled in the land we now call Israel. The Bible records a growing dispute between them and a simple form of resolution. They used no violence, no lawsuits, no lawyers, no courtrooms, and no judges. What could have escalated into broken family relationships, or even open warfare, was resolved by a simple, inexpensive, immediate procedure.

When it became apparent that there was not enough room for the followers of both men to stay in the same land, Abraham humbled himself and made the following offer:

> *So Abram said to Lot, "Let's not have any quarreling*
> *between you and me, or between your herdsmen and mine,*
> *for we are brothers.*
> *Is not the whole land before you?*
> *Let's part company.*
> *If you go to the left, I'll go to the right:*
> *if you go the right, I'll go to the left."*
> (Genesis 13:8–9)

Although this is similar to the procedure we now call "making a decision by lot," the real hero of the story is not Lot, who chose the best land that lay in the fertile Jordan valley. Instead, the credit goes to his uncle Abraham who cared more about his relationship with his nephew Lot than he did about getting the best property for himself.

Significantly, Lot's attempt to get the best for himself turned out to be the worst. Lot ended up in a city called Sodom near the Dead Sea, a city that was finally destroyed by God because of its decadence and corruption. As a result Lot lost his home, his wife, and much that he held dear (Genesis 13:10–13, 19).

By contrast, Abraham, who humbled himself and offered to take either portion that Lot did not want, ended up being blessed by God with wealth, honor, and a unique place in history as the

119

father of two great peoples we now know as Israel and Islam, as well as all the adopted children through Christ (Genesis 13:14–17, 15–16; Romans 4).

The Lot

This simple, quick, and inexpensive method of deciding issues by lot was often utilized by the Jews in the years that followed, usually for seemingly good purposes:

- Determining the territory to be allocated to certain tribes when the Israelites reached the promised land (Joshua 18:6).
- Deciding which men should fight (Judges 20:9).
- Deciding which families should minister at certain locations (1 Chronicles 26:13).
- Deciding who would replace Judas as a member of "the twelve" who followed Jesus (Acts 1:26).

This same simple method has been preserved down through the centuries. Children still decide today who gets a certain portion by drawing straws, and business partners divide companies by one side deciding the value and offering to buy or sell at the price he sets. The result has been the fast, effective, inexpensive resolution of conflicts and disputes for thousands of years.

We need to remember, however, that any gift can be used for good or for evil. The "lot" was no exception. For example, others used it to decide when to kill the Jews in captivity (Esther 3:7, 9:24), and to decide to throw Jonah overboard to calm a storm (Jonah 1:7).

120

The Lottery

Unfortunately, mankind has a way of turning a blessing into a blight whenever we allow our baser, selfish nature to gain control. It happens when we turn our competitive spirit away from fighting evil and into selfish ambition and self-centered desires. It happens when we take our special talents and gifts and use them merely for our own power and pleasure. And it also happens when we take God's gift of a simple way to resolve disputes and convert it into a game to try and gain wealth by engaging in chance.

Article 1, Section 3, of the original Kansas Constitution stated:

> "Lotteries and the sale of lottery tickets
> are *forever* prohibited"(emphasis added).

Gambling was also outlawed by statute. But *forever* didn't last. Society changed, the demand for public services and payments increased over the years, and state-controlled lotteries and other gambling became legal.

Today, the government itself has become a part of the gambling (now often renamed "gaming") it formerly banned as a crime! It's a short distance from good to evil. It often looks so good but can end up so sour!

I'm grateful our citizens said:

No!

From Grandpa With Love

Letter #9

Who Thanks Who?

"Never expect anyone to thank you," an older man quietly suggested to me one day as I was seeking perspective about the next chapter of my life. I pondered his statement from time to time over the years, but it wasn't until I compared two back-to-back stories in Luke 17 that I began to realize the depth of his comment. Studying these two accounts together also caused me to enlarge the principle to conclude that not only should we "never expect thanks," but, in addition, we should also "always give thanks."

Never Expect Thanks
The Case of the Unworthy Servant

In Luke 17:5 Jesus' disciples appealed to Him, "Increase our faith!" Part of His response was a surprising story (Luke 17:7–10):

Suppose one of you had a servant plowing or looking after the sheep.
Would he say to the servant when he comes in from the field,
"Come along now and sit down and eat?"
Would he not rather say, "Prepare my supper, get yourself ready,
and wait on me while I eat and drink;
after that you may eat and drink?"
Would he thank the servant because he did what he was told to do?
So you also, when you have done everything you were told to do,
should say, "We are unworthy servants;
we have only done our duty."

It seems clear that we are to do what we do because God has given us the assignment—not for personal reward, not for acclaim from the community, not even to feel the warm glow of a simple thank you. At first, this seems rather heartless, until we realize God will give us our true recognition-inheritance-reward in His own way and in His own good time.

We do what we do for God, without regard to the actions or reactions of our earthly masters. As the Apostle Paul puts it:

Whatever you do, work at it with all your heart,
as working for the Lord, not for men,
since you know that you will receive
an inheritance from the Lord as a reward.
It is the Lord you are serving.
(Colossians 3:23–24)

If we do what we do for earthly thanks, we are led to act first for those we serve, rather than for God. It isn't uncommon to receive carefully worded "thank-you letters" from organizations to whom we donate.

However, if we give only when we get the laudatory response we want, then the recipient, not God, controls our giving!

Always Give Thanks
The Case of the Thankful Leper

Immediately after the parable about never expecting thanks, Luke records an event showing Jesus' teaching that we should also always give thanks! As I read this second scripture, it seemed to validate the instructions I received early in my Christian life to give special attention to lists and sequences in the Bible, and to read more than a single scripture if we want to get balance from God's Word. Here's the story:

Now on his way to Jerusalem, Jesus traveled along the border between Samaria and Galilee.
As he was going into a village, ten men who had leprosy met him.
They stood at a distance and called out in a loud voice, "Jesus, Master, have pity on us!"
When he saw them, he said, "Go, show yourselves to the priests."
And as they went, they were cleansed.
One of them, when he saw he was healed, came back, praising God in a loud voice.
He threw himself at Jesus' feet and thanked him— and he was a Samaritan.
Jesus asked, "Were not all ten cleansed? Where are the other nine?
Was no one found to return and give praise to God except this foreigner?"
Then he said to him, "Rise and go; your faith has made you well."
(Luke 17:11–19)

In order to better understand this story, we first need to understand the difference between gratitude and thanks:

"Gratitude" is a feeling we *experience inwardly.*

"Thanks" is a fact we *express outwardly.*

The term gratitude (grateful, gratefulness) occurs only 3 times in the Bible. By contrast, the term thanks (thank, thankful, thanksgiving) appears over 100 times! God isn't simply trying to make us *feel* good. He also wants us to *act* good.

Feeling grateful only benefits me, but expressing thanks benefits us both, as well as serving as a model for others!

Whether or not we give thanks is not to be based on how well we like, or dislike, what is happening, nor because we feel good or bad, nor because it makes us comfortable or uncomfortable. Instead, we are to...

> *give thanks in all circumstances,*
> *for this is God's will for you in Christ Jesus.*
> (1 Thessalonians 5:18)

In other words, it is a simple act of obedience. We thank God and others because God wants us to do so.

So this is a letter of gratitude and thanksgiving. First, to God Who has blessed us all so greatly over all these years. Second, to each of you, and to all the others who have given time, talent, knowledge, material wealth, love, and their lives to me and to others—without ever expecting thanks in return. I am greatly in your debt.

May God Bless You All!

From Grandpa With Love

Letter #10

Who Do We Honor—and How?

I am fascinated by questions in the Bible. Such questions are often the key to principles or themes that God is teaching us throughout the scriptures. I am also drawn to the stories in the Bible that make a teaching come alive and memorable. And, best of all, is when God mixes together a memorable story and an intriguing question—and that is just what He does in the Old Testament book of Esther.

The Story

The principal characters in the story are the Persian King Xerxes; a young Jewish girl named Esther whom the king had chosen to be his new Queen; Mordecai, a Jewish relative of Esther who had recently saved the king from being assassinated; and Haman, second in command to the king, who would ultimately attempt to have all Jews in Persia killed and plundered, because of his hatred for Mordecai for refusing to pay homage to Him. When the king decided to honor Mordecai for helping to save the king's life, he asked the infamous Haman:

> *What should be done*
> *for the man the king delights to honor?*
> (Esther 6:6b)

Haman mistakenly thought the king was going to honor him, so he answered:

For the man the king delights to honor, have them bring a royal robe the king has worn and a horse the king has ridden, one with a royal crest placed on its head. Then let the robe and horse be entrusted to one of the king's noble princes. Let them robe the man the king delights to honor, and lead him on the horse through the city streets, proclaiming before him, "This is what is done for the man the king delights to honor!"
(Esther 6:7–9)

The king, with ironic, almost poetic justice, answered Haman:

Go at once…Get the robe and the horse and do just as you have suggested for Mordecai the Jew, who sits at the king's gate. Do not neglect anything you have recommended.
(Esther 6:10)

Deeply humiliated, Haman complied. Mordecai was honored, Haman was shamed and ultimately hanged, God saved the Jews, and the Feast of Purim is still celebrated by Jews in recognition of and thanksgiving to God for their salvation.

The king's question about honor is only a supporting issue for the main story, but it caught my attention, so I began to pursue the question.

As I looked back, I realized that honor had played a significant role in my *physical* world over the years. For example:

Scout Oath—"On my honor I will do my best…"
Schools—The "Honor Roll" for those who excel.

Marriage Vows—"to love, honor..."
Law Practice—"Your Honor," referring to the Judge.
Funerals for Military and Veterans—"Honor guard"

But honor was not consciously emphasized in my spiritual life. It surprised me, therefore, to learn that the word "honor" appeared in the Bible more often than many common terms, such as grace and baptism. *In fact, honor was mentioned (and sometimes commanded) over 150 times!*

And it always seemed to indicate a lifting up, respect, and recognition of the highest and best—including Heaven for God, Thrones for Kings, and the Head of the Table for those who were important.

So I asked myself what should be done for each of these I am told to honor? Here are some conclusions based on verses about honor and related scriptures, plus a lifetime of memories:

Honor God (I Timothy 1:17; John 5:23; 1 Corinthians 6:20)
- Always put God first in what we think, say, and do.
- Openly follow Jesus and obey His commands.
- Give Him the first and the best.
- Celebrate His special days and events.
- Never do or say anything that will bring Him shame.

Honor Marriage (Hebrews 13:4; Ephesians 5:22–33)
- Commit to marriage openly before God and His people.
- Keep the marriage vows.
- Carry out the Biblical roles for husbands, wives, and parents.
- Encourage lifetime Christian marriage as a way of life.
- Celebrate Mother's Day, Father's Day, and Anniversaries,

Honor Parents (Exodus 20:12; Ephesians 6:2)
- Obey them when we are young.
- Live Godly lives and retain good family relationships.
- Celebrate special days and events in their lives.
- Give them dignity, help, and respect when they are older.
- Provide Christian burial and remembrance when they die.

Honor Civil Authorities (Romans 13:6–7; 1 Peter 2:17)
- Acknowledge them as God's servants.
- Obey them (secularly) unless they violate God's commands.
- Pray for them privately and publically.
- Celebrate days and events of public importance.

Honor Elders (I Timothy 5:17; Philippians 2:29)
- Recognize their position through public installation.
- Obey them (religiously) unless they violate God's commands.
- Pray for them privately and publically.
- Provide for their needs and encourage them.

Honor Believers (Romans 12:10; Philippians 2:3; I Corinthians 12:23–24)
- Consider others better than ourselves.
- Extol others' spiritual gifts, especially the quiet gifts.
- Help, encourage, and pray for one another throughout life.
- Celebrate the accomplishments and special events of others.

It has been helpful to consider these various scriptures and situations. There are many more. But if I had to give my answer to the King's question in a few words, it would be these:

**Lift up, respect, and give recognition
to God and others!**

From Grandpa With Love

Letter #11

How Can I Better Understand The Bible?

As a youngster, I tried more than once to start at Genesis and read through the Bible. Each time I gave up in frustration after battling page after page of thee's, thou's, sacrifices, feasts, and long lists of people and places I couldn't identify or even pronounce.

Now, as an oldster, I find much of the Bible is still a mystery, but over the years the Holy Spirit has provided various teachers and insights that have helped me (as a layman) come closer to its Truth. Hopefully, the 12 tips below will help you, too.

As usual, hold on to what is good (of God)—and discard the rest.

1. Being a Believer
The Bible is written from a Father to His children. Don't expect to comprehend its message until you are part of the family. That happens when we totally surrender to Him and accept Jesus as His Son (John 1:12). And don't expect nonbelievers to understand much, nor to teach much truth from the Bible (2 Peter 2:1).

2. Use the Bible as a Library
The word "Bible" comes from the term "book," but it actually contains 66 books written by dozens of writers over hundreds of years. The Old Testament has 5 books of Law, 12 books of History, 5 books of Poetry, and 17 books of Prophecy. The New Testament has 4 books about the life of Jesus, 1 book about the Acts of the Apostles, 21 Letters, and ends with 1 book of Prophecy. Together they carry God's message to all those who

are willing to be taught, reproved, corrected, and trained (2 Timothy 3:16–17).

3. Value Form As Well As Substance
God has chosen to create our world using visible form (Genesis 1:1). The Bible didn't simply come together automatically. It was placed in writing and then compiled in its form for a reason. Form is the bucket that carries the water. If we lose the bucket, the water is poured out onto the sand and disappears. Placing the Bible in writing, and compiling it in an orderly form, has allowed our faith to be transmitted from generation to generation over thousands of years.

4. Compare Translations and Commentaries
Many believe the Bible is inerrant in the original, but it is clear those who translate it into other languages and those who give their interpretation of the meanings of various scriptures are not. One way to test for both of these possible errors is to read various translations and commentaries. The Bible tells us, "As iron sharpens iron, so one man sharpens another" (Proverbs 27:17).

5. Read Scriptures Before Commentaries
It is tempting to become a clone, unless we hear what the Holy Spirit says to us when we read and study a passage, before we compare it with commentators who tell us what He has shown them.

6. Get an Overview of the Whole Bible
Individual scriptures are more understandable, as well as more accurately applied, when we see how they fit into the overall thrust of God's Word. It helps to view the Bible first as a globe before we descend to look at specific hills and valleys.

7. Rely on Themes
The Bible will often prove itself, by itself. Look for the great themes that repeatedly appear throughout the Bible. Be careful about isolated scriptures that don't follow the great messages (1 John 3:11; 2 John 5–6)

8. Be Aware of Context
Enjoy the uniqueness of different times, places, and cultures, as well as the backgrounds of the writers and the needs and characteristics of the audiences. For example, differences in the four accounts of the Gospel, written by four diverse men to four diverse groups, don't pose a problem as much as they display God's vastness!

9. Watch for Last Messages
Messages written shortly before death often summarize and/or emphasize what God has given the writer to pass on to others. For example, look at Deuteronomy, written by Moses shortly before his death; Ecclesiastes, believed to have been written by Solomon as an old man; the "Upper Room Discourse" of Jesus (John 13–17), which took place shortly before His crucifixion; and 2 Timothy and 2 Peter, written by Paul and Peter in anticipation of their deaths.

10. Study Sequences, Lists, and Repetition
Early on I was advised to watch for sequences and lists in the Bible. When I read the list of the "acts of the sinful nature" and then compare it with the "fruit of the Spirit," in Galatians 5, the stark contrast is unforgettable. And when I read in 1 Kings 12 the tragic account of the never-reconciled split in the Hebrew nation, which resulted from the erroneous actions of a new king who relied on the counsel of young men instead of the more Godly wisdom of the

elders, it teaches me a strong life lesson—which becomes doubly important when I find it repeated in 2 Chronicles 10!

11. Balance Truth

Some of God's Truth needs to be balanced with other parts of His Truth. For example, competing doctrines—such as the Sovereignty of God and the Free Will of Man; and Faith and Works—each have multiple passages that support their position. Our earthbound view is small; God's view is infinite. I believe He can hold two views we see as incompatible—and that many Biblical disputes will ultimately be resolved by both/and rather than either/or (Isaiah 55:8–9).

12. Remain Teachable

The Holy Spirit has much to show us, but we must be willing to learn. It is sometimes necessary, but humbling, to learn from people or incidents we would rather do without. I encourage you to never stop learning, particularly from teachers who are still searching themselves. Test carefully those who are overly certain they already know God's will and meaning—especially as it pertains to what others should do.

In closing, let me encourage you to be content to "know in part" the Ways and the Word of God. Someday we will "know fully," but for now we must be content with what God allows us to comprehend and then trust Him with the rest (I Corinthians 13:12).

If we could know it all, we would be God—and we aren't!

From Grandpa With Love

Letter #12

What Do I Really Believe?

For God so loved the world that he gave his one and only Son,
that whoever believes in him shall not perish
but have eternal life.
(John 3:16)

August 10, 2009

I was born 84 years ago today—and "born again" 44 years later. During the next few minutes let me walk with you through some of those years that, hopefully, may be of some help in your own life journey.

On July 22, 1959 (a few days before my 34th birthday), alone in my office, I typed out a rather lengthy statement of my beliefs, entitled it "This I Believe"—and then carefully placed the pages in the back of my file cabinet so no one else would know my inner thoughts!

As I recently reread these fifty year old pages (now somewhat fragile and starting to yellow around the edges), I thought how those beliefs subtly, yet dramatically, changed during the next ten years, causing me to make a decision on August 10, 1969, that would alter my life for eternity.

Below is my 1959 Belief Statement (as refined two years later on August 20, 1961), together with some comments and a series of scriptures showing some of what the Bible says about "believing." As you read further, you will see why, since August 10, 1969, I like the last list better.

This I Believe

(July 22, 1959; August 20, 1961)

I.   *I believe in God.*

II.   *I believe in right and wrong; that right will be rewarded and wrong punished.*

III.   *I believe in forgiveness, but not in place of punishment.*

IV.   *I believe in Jesus Christ as the earthly manifestation of God.*

V.   *I believe that God, through the Holy Ghost, appears in each person to the extent we will allow—and that "love" is the outward sign of this inward appearance.*

VI.   *I believe that God has given life purpose, both for individuals and for mankind as a whole.*

VII.   *I believe that "Thy Kingdom come, thy will be done, on earth as it is in Heaven" is the clearest explanation of God's goal for civilization; and that man's purpose as an individual is to help in the achievement of this "Heaven on Earth" while living in such manner as to pass to a spiritual Heaven after death.*

VIII.   *I believe that this goal can be attained only by the use of all our peculiar talents.*

IX.   *I believe that true happiness is really fulfillment, and that we reach this fulfillment to the degree that we use our abilities and help others use theirs.*

X.   *I believe that man, collectively and individually, is opposed by deterrents or brakes—and that we must overcome these drags to fulfill our purpose and reach our goal—In effect, that we must **do,** not merely **be.***

XI.   *I believe that civilization's rate of movement toward this "Heaven on Earth" depends on each generation's degree of fulfillment.*

XII.   *I believe that our forward movement, as opposed, causes us to move forward unsteadily, from peak to peak, but each higher than the last.*

XIII.   *I believe that we hold an inner urge to use our abilities to fill a void; that these lacks are God's challenges to us to progress toward our goals; and that as we overcome each lack we as individuals reach new peaks, also.*

XIV.   *I believe that among the most serious of the deterrents we meet are temptations to stray from moderation.*

XV.   *I believe that people are tempted to stray from moderation and toward excess in different areas—and that what tempts one may hold no threat for another—and that no one can fully appreciate the temptations or drags of another.*

XVI.   *I believe that each person's fulfillment is proportional to his success in over-coming his drags and thus putting his abilities to fullest use.*

XVII.   *I believe that each ability carries with it an obligation, and that much of man's problems come from failure to accept and carry out his responsibility.*

XVIII.   *I believe that man is making progress toward its goal— and that one of the surest evidences of such progress is the codification and use of God's laws as revealed through individuals.*

XIX.   *I believe that God moves in natural, not unnatural, ways, keeping in mind that the unknown of today is the known of tomorrow*

XX. *I believe that man must explore all of this unknown as a part of his upward aim, and that all the universe—both larger and smaller—is God's physical goal for men.*

Reflections

After longing and intermittingly searching for God and the purpose of life most of my young life, there were some worthwhile conclusions in my rather wordy statement. But I was wrong in one major area—and it was summarized in Article VII, which I mistakenly believed was the key that would open the door to a Utopian "Heaven on Earth" and give me entrance into a "spiritual Heaven" when I died. How wrong I was! My error not only contaminated much of the rest of the statement, but it also kept me from the Truth for many years.

In looking back on my Belief Statement, I am reminded of two major characters in the Old Testament: Job and Solomon. Job believed he was a righteous man who was trying to follow God. It seemed unfair to him that God would allow him to lose his family, his wealth, and his health without ever giving Job a reason for the disasters. It took Job 37 chapters of trouble and a long message from God before he finally came to the conclusion he voices in Job 42:3b, 5–6:

> *Surely I spoke of things too wonderful for me to know...*
> *My ears had heard of you, but now my eyes have seen you.*
> *Therefore I despise myself and repent in dust and ashes.*

While Solomon did not have the troubles of Job, he did acquire riches and fame and became one of the wisest, wealthiest, most powerful monarchs of his time. But, after telling about his...

great projects...houses...gardens and parks...male and female slaves...
more herds and flocks than anyone in Jerusalem
before me...silver and gold for myself,
and the treasure of kings and provinces...
(Ecclesiastes 2:4–9)

Solomon concludes it was all "meaningless, a chasing after the wind," a refrain he repeats eight other times during the book. Finally, he concludes:

Now all has been heard; here is the conclusion of the matter:
Fear God and keep his commandments,
for this is the whole duty of man.
(Ecclesiastes 12:13)

Both men started out believing life revolved around them, as most of us seem to do in our earlier years. Both men ultimately submitted to God, just as I would ultimately do.

When I wrote "This I Believe" 50 years ago, it was based largely on what I and all the others in this world should *do* or not *do*. Nowhere did I speak of the need to believe in Jesus as the Christ and Son of God who came and died on the Cross in order that I and others might be redeemed and made whole! I obviously felt at that time that our works were the key. It was as if God put the world together and then it was up to us to make it all work out right (which we believed we could do)—and it was also up to us to live so we could get into Heaven when we die.

The result was a treadmill that seemed to go faster and faster, resulting in ever-increasing stress, as I tried to live up to what I believed.

A New Belief Statement
For the next few years I wrestled with God. Gradually, I began to realize that it was a test of the will. Either God's will or my will was going to rule my life, and it had to be total, unconditional surrender.

Finally, on August 10, 1969, my 44th birthday (10 years after I had typed the first "This I Believe" statement), I knelt alone in our bedroom and confessed something like this:

> "Lord, I commit all of myself to you that I am able,
> and I accept Jesus as your divine Son."

My goal had changed from trying to work my way through life and into Heaven, to submitting to God and trusting Him to take me where He wanted me to go—now and forever!

Below are a few of the Scriptures (emphasis added) that have helped me to see what to believe, from *God's* perspective:

1. *Yet to all who received him, to those who **believed** in his name, he gave the right to become children of God—* (John 1:12)

2. *For God so loved the world that he gave his one and only Son, that whoever **believes** in him shall not perish but have eternal life* (John 3:16).

3. *Then they asked him, "What must we do to do the works God requires?" Jesus answered, "The work of God is this: to **believe** the one he sent"* (John 6:28–29).

4. *The jailer called for lights, rushed in and fell trembling before Paul and Silas. He brought them out and asked, "Sirs, what must I do to be saved?" They replied, "**Believe** in the Lord Jesus, and you will be saved—you and your household"* (Acts 16:29–31).

5. *That if you confess with your mouth, "Jesus is Lord," and **believe** in your heart that God raised him from the dead, you will be saved. For it is with your heart that you **believe** and are justified, and it is with your mouth that you confess and are saved* (Romans 10:9–10).

6. *Though you have not seen him, you love him; and even though you do not see him now, you **believe** in him and are filled with an inexpressible and glorious joy, for you are receiving the goal of your faith, the salvation of your souls* (1 Peter 1:8–9).

Believing in Jesus is such an integral part of our faith that followers of Jesus were referred to as "believers" 20 times in the New Testament—compared to only three times when they were referred to as "Christians"!

It has now been forty years since I first surrendered and accepted Jesus on August 10, 1969. As I look back, I see that it was just the first of many surrenders we are called to make if we want God to be in charge—of our world, our family, our work, our money, our health, and on and on.

Each time it is a struggle; but each time we submit, it becomes more and more clear that God does not need what we can do for Him, nearly as much as we need to believe in Him and allow Him to carry out His will in and through our lives.

History indicates Jesus was about age 33—and perfect—when He died. I was age 33 when I wrote my 1959 statement—and how little I really knew! But God is gracious. Once we surrender, He will guide us and instruct us in the way *He* wants us to go. I was stressed and unsure the first 44 years on my own. It has been so much better the last forty years, relying on Him and His Word for directions.

I mentioned in the personal note at the beginning that, after I wrote "This I Believe" in 1959, I "...carefully placed the pages in the back of my file cabinet so that no one else would know my inner thoughts!" That all changed after my confession on August 10, 1969. I came to realize that "good news" is not for hiding or hoarding. We need to share it with others if we really care about them and want the best for them.

That is why I am sending you this letter. I pray it will encourage you in your own faith journey. I hope it will also encourage you that it often takes many years for our faith to mature. Sometimes we have flashes of insight; at other times our faith seems more like a flower that gradually opens up. Sometimes there are long periods of dormancy just as there were during the 400-year intervals between the Patriarchs and the Exodus, and again between the Old Testament and the New Testament.

But after all these years, I realize we will never fully understand all God is saying to us until we finally get to Heaven. When I arrive, I hope to be like Grandma, who said her first words would be, "Oh! Thank you! Thank you for letting me come!"

After that, I expect to exclaim what another man told me he would probably say: "Oh! *Now* I see!" What a celebration that will be.

See You There!

From Grandpa With Love

Letter #13

Ten Basic Principles

Below are ten Basic Principles I wrote (in the early 1970s as near as I can recall). Since much of it has served me well for almost forty years, I thought you might like to have a copy. It is not perfect, and it does not cover everything, but I pray it is helpful. As always, hold on to what is good (of God)—and discard the rest.

1. Put First Things First
Put Christ first, wife second, children third, and others (such as employer, friends, etc.) last. Mixing up this order is disastrous, and until this order is put into effect, it seems the rest of life is disorderly.

2. Accept Yourself
God made you as He wanted you for the job He has for you. He loves you, so love and accept yourself. Watch your grooming, language, and conduct so these will not detract from the real you.

3. Accept Others
The best definition I know of real love in action is "Accept others as they are; give them what they need (not what they want)." By contrast, lust means to use others to give me what I want. Love gives life; lust kills.

4. Take The Ball
Accept leadership when it is handed to you; be willing to follow when it is not. Learning to be a good subordinate is a major

element in preparing to be a good leader. Serve those you lead; obey those you follow. Be the spiritual, physical, and financial head of your family.

5. Be Free
Ask forgiveness of those you offend; forgive those who offend you before they ask. This will keep you free from bitterness and self-pity.

6. Live With A Margin
For example, keep a little gas in your tank and a little money in the bank. Learn to start a little early, and save a little energy for emergencies. This lifestyle helps keep you in control, instead of being controlled. We can either discipline ourselves, or others will do it for us.

7. Be Wise
God's way is often upside down from doing what comes naturally. The best method of finding His way is through scripture. I suggest you read one chapter of Proverbs each day for a month (there are 31 chapters). Then repeat this procedure for six months. Gradually move to other portions of scripture for reading, study, and meditation. Follow the spirit more than the letter of what you read. You will never be the same again. Wisdom begins with fearing God; it is completed by loving Him—and others—and yourself.

8. Don't Chase The Wind
Decide your life work and what you will need to accomplish it. Be sure it is worth trading your life for it. In everything you do, consider this formula:

- Write out your goal;
- Write out your plan (procedure) to get there;
- Work hard.

Planning ahead is one of the major keys to success. But remember, you are not the final authority; accept God's changes for your life when they occur.

9. Understand Finance
Financial difficulty is a major cause of unhappiness and divorce. Have your career well planned before you take on the responsibility of a family. After you make the money, spend some, save some, and give some. Let your wife be responsible for increasing the money you provide. In general, don't borrow for depreciating assets.

10. Respect Time
Your time is limited; use it wisely. There is a proper time for everything. For example, always build your foundation first. If you try to go fast and build on sand, the project often fails, and you have to waste time by starting over.

From Grandpa With Love

Letter #14

Asking Our Elders

Moses, in his final song at the end of Deuteronomy (about 1500 BC), gave this advice:

> *Remember the days of old; consider the generations long past.*
> *Ask your father and he will tell you,*
> *your elders, and they will explain to you.*
> (Deuteronomy 32:7)

And when Socrates spoke (around 500 BC) to Cephalus, he is reported to have said:

> *There is nothing which for my part I like better, Cephalus, than*
> *conversing with aged men; for I regard them as travelers who have*
> *gone on a journey which I too may have to go, and of whom I ought to*
> *inquire whether the way is smooth and easy,*
> *or rugged and difficult...*

I have determined that those of us who want to receive all God has for us need to humble ourselves and become spiritual beggars. *We must cast all our pride and false egoism aside and ask—particularly those who have gone ahead of us!*

In my boyhood and younger adult life, I sometimes asked questions and sought answers from those older than I. But it wasn't until I reached my 40s that I began a pattern of seeking out elders with specific requests for time alone to give me advice and perspective.

Sometimes it has meant calling a person I didn't know. At other times the request was to someone so much older and wiser that it seemed presumptuous even to ask. But virtually all have responded generously, and seemed genuinely pleased to share lessons they have learned on their journey. A few examples of what I learned are set forth below.

Asking A 70-Year-Old

I was looking for new direction during my 40s. Since I knew no older spiritual grandfather figure locally, I decided to call three men whose writings had helped me. I couldn't reach two of them, but my third call, to a widely known writer, speaker, pastor, and professor at a small Christian college hit pay dirt. He seemed much older at the time, so he was probably in his 70s.

Although I was totally unknown to him, he welcomed my call and invited me to come for a visit. He prepared a guest room for me, and then spent the entire next day answering my questions and helping me sort out the direction my life should now take. I'll never forget his opening comment that was so unusual in our hurried, harried world:

"We have time! Isn't that wonderful? We have time!"

He gave me his undivided attention that day, and several other times over the years—when I asked.

He was the first to encourage me to write and offered to critique my work, which began my effort to relate the teachings of Jesus and the Bible to everyday life. And he helped me comprehend some of the power and lasting effect of writing when he told me:

> "You can walk with the greats.
> All you have to do is to take them off the shelves."

His counsel and encouragement have been invaluable.

Asking An 80-Year-Old

Another older man who helped me had walked with some of the giants of the corporate and religious worlds. I first met him when I asked to take him to the airport following his speaking engagement in Wichita. During our short visit, I discovered he was about ten years my senior. Some years later, as I approached my 70s and felt the need to inquire about what might lie ahead, I called and asked if we could meet again. He quickly agreed.

I invited one of my teenage grandsons to go along, and told him, "Come along and you can learn what you need to know for your 70s." I had to smile at his honest reply: "But Grandpa, I don't think I'll remember!"

We flew down to our host's city and met with him 2 or 3 hours. Here's what we heard:

> *First*: Learn to manage deterioration. It has been exciting to expand. Now we must learn the difficult art of contraction.

Second: Concentrate on the core items of life: Health, Wealth, Relationships, and Usefulness. We don't need unlimited amounts of any of these four items, only enough to be and do what God has planned for this season of our life.

Third: When I asked if there were any surprises, he replied, "Yes. It was much harder than I expected!"

Our talk was brief. But I found myself returning to his comments again and again as I moved through this decade.

Asking Some 90-Year-Olds

Recently I have spoken with several 90-year-olds. When I asked one, "How do you like being 93?" he answered simply, "Eighty-nine was better!"

And after I complimented him on his writings, he noted, "Writing is God's gift to an old man!"

When I told another, "I graduated from Wichita East High in 1943." She responded, "Oh, I graduated in 1925!" A few weeks later I attended her 100th birthday party—and not long afterward, I saw her working out in a fitness center!

But most of us who reach these older years will face physical and/ or mental challenges. One man brought it poignantly home as he spoke lovingly of his wheelchair-bound wife of many years: "Freedom isn't being able to drive...but to walk." Then he added, "When you can't sleep together, get adjoining recliner chairs so you can hold hands at night."

I profited greatly in some way from every conversation!

Asking A Centenarian

The peak of my requests went to an alert, vigorous, 101-year-old man actively engaged in the profession he began over 75 years ago. Our hour together was a treasure time!

He began by saying that no one can tell others how to live. But his stories of his beloved blind father, revered mother, and a life of hard work enriched my perspective about life.

He was "now" oriented and content to deal with the problems he faced each day, rather than worrying about the past or the future. He was courteous, kind, and complimentary to me and others in his life. He was grateful about life and all those who had helped him along the way.

No advice, but much to learn and ponder. And when I left, he smiled and said, "Come back any time. I'm still learning!"

A Final Note

God has granted me an untold wealth of wisdom from countless older men and women. Some help came because I made specific requests, such as those listed above. Some help came through ordinary conversations and watching how others lived. To all of them, I say, "Thanks!"

Let me close with this final thought. Jesus told his disciples,

Ask and it will be given to you;
Seek and you will find;

> *knock and the door will be opened to you.*
> (Matthew 7:7)

But he also warned against *false* teachers:

> *Watch out for false prophets. They come to you in sheep's clothing,*
> *but inwardly they are ferocious wolves.*
> *By their fruit you will recognize them.*
> *Do people pick grapes from thorn bushes or figs from thistles?*
> *Likewise, every good tree bears good fruit,*
> *but a bad tree bears bad fruit.*
> *A good tree cannot bear bad fruit,*
> *and a bad tree cannot bear good fruit.*
> *Every tree that does not bear good fruit is cut down*
> *and thrown into the fire.*
> *Thus by their fruit you will recognize them.*
> (Matthew 7:15–20)

And He reminded them in Luke 6:40:

> *A student is not above his teacher,*
> *but everyone who is fully trained will be like his teacher.*

So I encourage you to seek out older people whose lives have produced the kind of "good fruit" you want to flow in and through your life, and then "ask."

You meet a lot of nice folks.
You often get real wisdom.
And you may save yourself a lot of steps—and scars!

From Grandpa With Love

Letter #15

How Can We Share Our Faith With The World Around Us?

How beautiful are the feet of those who bring good news.
(Romans 10:15b)

Most of us are reluctant to speak out about our core beliefs. But as you will see from the following remarks, it is ordinary people like you and me whom God has chosen to carry faith in Him to our generation, and to those who follow us.

Some years ago I began to understand that God gives the gift of evangelism to *some* believers, but Jesus made it clear we are *all* to be His witnesses:

But you will receive power when the Holy Spirit comes on you;
and you will be my witnesses
in Jerusalem, and in all Judea and Samaria,
and to the ends of the earth.
(Acts 1:8)

Whether it is proper or not to witness about our faith has become a hot topic in our society. Our belief system forms the value base for most of our decisions. It is why we do what we do. While our faith is a personal decision, I have concluded it cannot be separated and placed in a vacuum, to be discussed only in the privacy of a church or home.

Earlier generations understood this as they acknowledged "Our Creator" in the Declaration of Independence and "Almighty God" in the Kansas Constitution, took oaths based upon "God," and engraved Biblical quotations on our public buildings.

Every life here on earth constantly involves faith and what we believe. Even more importantly, our destiny for eternity is affected by our faith. The issue is not whether we have faith, but in what or whom shall we place our faith. And the decisions we make and share with others (or fail to share with others) will affect our lives and the lives of those around us in this world, and for eternity.

While we are commanded to witness outward "to the ends of the earth," *the simplest and most effective means of passing our faith is to our own children, grandchildren, and great-grandchildren!* A cursory look at every civilization in history reveals that most people follow in the faith of their parents. Thus, when we begin our "witnessing" in our own "Jerusalem," i.e., in our own home to our own family, we carry out God's principal method of passing His faith.

What we do and what we say (or fail to do and say) to those around us is the primary witness for most of us. But we can also leave an important witness in writing, as Biblical writers and saints have done for us. How poor we would be if we had no *written* record from those who went before us!

On January 1, 1876, Sarah Jane Cook, the great-great-great-great-grandmother of our great-grandchildren wrote the following statement on an ordinary sheet of tablet paper:

I consecrate myself afresh to God, today, laying all upon the altar with a full determination to ever lean upon Jesus and follow Him, and with God's help to lead a new life. And also with a full determination to pray more earnestly for my boys. God help me.

—Sarah Jane Cook

She died on January 26, 1876, just 26 days later!

For years that framed piece of ordinary tablet paper with those priceless words hung on our bedroom wall. Little did Sarah Jane Cook know her simple witness would encourage her descendants for decades after she was gone!

**It is my prayer that we will all be faithful witnesses for Christ
to those around us
—particularly to those of our own family—
including a written record for those who follow us!**

From Grandpa With Love

Letter #16

How Shall I Face Growing Older?

Some years ago, a younger (than I) woman who had been dealing with the problem of aging, said rather contentedly, "I fought turning 40. I embraced turning 50!"

After turning not only 40 and 50 but also 60, 70, and 80, I conclude she is right.

It's OK to grow older, as long as we learn to *embrace* the advancing years. Ecclesiastes 3 says there is "a time to be born and time to die." But it also says God "made everything beautiful in its time." That *has* to include *old* age. In fact I have found that in many ways, life gets richer each year.

If people don't want to grow older, they must think this world is better than Heaven, since old age, for most of us, is the gateway to Heaven!

Looking Ahead

I no longer believe "Time began when I was born and will end when I die." I think we can see ahead about as far as we have lived. So I am trying to look ahead 82 years to AD 2089 and into eternity, and pass on what I get to those who are here today and those who are following. I want to be like Jeremiah who bought property as he planned ahead for his family to return from captivity after seventy years—not like Hezekiah, who received fifteen years of extra life, and when he learned that his kingdom would fall after his death, thought,

> *Will there not be peace and security in **my** lifetime?"*
> (2 Kings 20:19, emphasis added)

Word Working

God made me a word worker. But now I write shorter. As Ecclesiastes 6:11 says:

> *The more the words, the less the meaning,*
> *and how does that profit anyone?*

In earlier years I wrote legal briefs and contracts, a few small books, and a number of booklets. Now I am writing short little letters I have entitled "Letters From Grandpa" to our family and some friends. I'm finding many like these better!

I no longer say "author." Author means *we* create, i.e., *we* have authority. Since God creates it all, I like the term "writer." Because the writings are not mine, I can distribute them free of charge, including a website. Since I want these to circulate as widely as God wants, the only restriction is that others are asked not to change the writings or charge for copies. Many people like that better, too.

Advising

I don't give much specific advice now. Advisors need to know all the facts as well as the context and circumstances. This becomes increasingly difficult as we age and new generations are in charge. I believe my principal job now is to provide love, continuity, and a sense of perspective from life and the Bible for those seeking answers.

Becoming Children

I was told that the trip through the birth canal is terribly hard. It's probably good we don't remember. The trip through the final road into Heaven is also often hard, but the goal is worth it. Jesus impressed on us the need to be "like a little child." Life starts simple, gets more complex, and then goes back to simple. As we age we get rid of lots of fluff. We get down to the essence. The years remove much of the dross. Maybe that's why we sometimes call our older years a second childhood.

Receiving

We all start our lives as receivers. We are totally helpless and dependent on others when we enter this world. It seems natural for a child to receive. But, by adulthood, we often become givers. Many know Acts 20:35:

It is more blessed to give than to receive.

It is also more fun! There is nothing as exhilarating as being the giver. But it can build pride. By contrast, receiving is very humbling.

Although we start life as receivers, once we have known the thrill—and sometimes the power—of giving, it often becomes very difficult for us to humble ourselves and be the receivers. That is one of the reasons we fight growing older. We dread being humbled and increasingly forced to be dependent and receive from others, like a little child.

But receiving is as important as giving. It is part of what makes life have value. *If we ever eliminate all the poor, sick, elderly, imprisoned, and needy, we will eliminate love from the world. Because every act of love requires not only a lover but also a lovee!*

So I must play my part, sometimes as a giver, and sometimes as a receiver. And there are times the latter may be the most important!

Letting Go

Sometimes I feel like I'm in an airport waiting for them to call my flight! I've found one key to contentment is being willing to let go of everything: our bodies, minds, abilities, status, usefulness, money, as well as our old friends and our loved ones, and then truly being grateful for whatever we still have left each day (Matthew 6:33–34).

Paradoxically, Grandma and I repeatedly say this is one of the best times of our lives. We are not so bothered by the big things the world thinks are important, and we can concentrate on the things that God says are important: "God, His Love and His Word, and People!"

So, I encourage you: embrace growing older!
It's kind of nice to get back to the simple things,
and then receive the Kingdom of God like a little child.
(Luke 18:17)

From Grandpa With Love

Part V

The Gift of "Receiving"

For who makes you different from anyone else?
What do you have that you did not receive?
And if you did receive it, why do you boast
as though you did not?
(1 Corinthians 4:7)

Preface

2008

The following comments were prepared for a Prayer Breakfast in Wichita, Kansas, my hometown. The request was simply that I reflect back on life and what I had learned that I would like to pass on.

The trip through a lifetime of memories overwhelmed me with gratitude and thanks to God and to each person and group He has used to give me so much for so many years. I pray that placing these reflections in writing will now allow the gifts to increase and flow into and through the lives of others, so God will be glorified and the givers and receivers will be blessed.

But, remember, we all err, so test what I say, hold on to what is good (of God)—and discard the rest.

May God richly bless you as you walk with Him through life.

From Grandpa With Love

The Gift of "Receiving"

As I walk back through 82 years of memories, one significant theme keeps emerging. It is summarized by three short questions in 1 Corinthians 4:7:

> *For who makes you different from anyone else?*
> *What do you have that you did not receive?*
> *And if you did receive it, why do you boast*
> *as though you did not?*

In other words, we all are on a common journey; we are all receivers, and since we are all receivers, there is no reason ever to boast (to others or even to ourselves) about what we do with what we have been given.

I realize now life has been one long gift, and I have discovered that the humbling, often unrecognized gift that underlies all God's other gifts is the ability to receive. *It has totally changed my life to realize I do not start as a giver but as a receiver, who is simply given the opportunity and responsibility to enjoy, increase, and then distribute God's gifts in His name, after I receive!*

From the time I can remember, it has always been emphasized that I was to love others. Finally, in 1975, at the age of 49, I received a lesson showing me that giving didn't start with me, but with God! It came through a good friend who told me what I needed to hear, even when I didn't want to receive it. We were at a Christian bookstore when I saw a particular book that appealed to me, and I mentioned it to my friend. He said, "Let me buy it for you."

I declined and indicated I would get it myself. He responded, "Oh, come on, let me buy you the book." Instead of graciously accepting his offer, I insisted I would buy the book. He simply smiled and waited until I returned from paying. Then he said, "Here, let me write in it." I handed it to him but thought how strange that he wanted to write in the flyleaf when I had bought the book. When he handed it back to me, I opened the book and read the following statement:

"To Marvin, From Marvin, In Love"

followed by my friend's signature. Now would you like to know the name of the book I had bought for myself? It was

Let God Love You!

During the next few minutes, I would like to tell you about a few of God's love gifts that have blessed my life, *once I was willing to receive them.* There are many, many more, but hopefully these will make the point. Obviously, His gifts are to be enjoyed, increased, and passed on to others; but today, I am going to concentrate on receiving from God, since this is where all giving begins. In order to keep us together on our journey, I'll give a brief synopsis of each decade in my life and then tie in some personal illustrations.

1920s *The Gift of Life*

We all enter life at a certain time and place that we do not control. We have nothing to do with when we are born, where we are born, or to whom we are born. We do not choose our gender, race, color, or ethnic background, or our ancestors' reputation or economic status. We do not choose our early models, good or bad. Neither do we have any control over our early training or discipline, or our lack of them. We have nothing to do with the mind, body, or emotions we receive at birth. These are all "givens" in our lives.

Sometimes we are prone to speak of someone who rises to prominence out of difficult beginnings as a self-made person. But when we look deeply, we usually find inherent qualities that, while laudably used, were often based on a set of "givens" over which he or she had no control.

I received life in Wesley hospital in 1925 in the middle of the Roaring Twenties, which ended with the stock market crash of 1929. The first home I remember was at First and Oliver. The street was half paved. We had a barn, a cow, and warm milk I could receive straight from the cow into my cup. My parents sacrificed, and worked to instill faith, love, discipline, a work ethic, and respect for the lives and property of others. I didn't earn any of it. It was a gift. And it was ancestors before me who lived and worked and built this nation who gave me the opportunity to speak, worship, work, and live where I want. All I did was to receive. Then it was up to me to enjoy, increase, and pass on what I was given.

Little children receive easily and naturally. Watch their unbounded joy at Christmastime; there is no sense of repayment or guilt. Just joy at receiving! As we age, it seems to get more complicated. Some say we don't appreciate anything unless we earn it. And we only value what costs us something. *If that is true, we don't value most of what we have, because most of it is a gift!*

From whom I receive my life is a foundational issue. If my life is a gift from God, that is reason to submit to and follow Him. It is also reason to follow His command:

> *Be fruitful and increase in number...*
> (Genesis 1:28)

and to treat each person, including the unborn and the very old and feeble, as sacred, since we are all made in the image of God. If I simply evolved out of nothing, then I am my own god and I make my own rules and follow my own desires.

Determining the origin of life sets the stage for everything else we believe and do during our years here on earth.

1930s *The Gift of Growing Up*

The 1930s were the decade of the Great Depression. In 1932, at age 7, I moved to ten acres on North Arkansas that we called simply, "The Farm." We had cows, pigs, chickens, and a pony. I attended a two-room school, with a teacher I dearly loved. It all cost me nothing. All I had to do was receive.

One summer, I attended old Camp Hyde. I think it cost $5.00 a week. The Arkansas River was our swimming hole. One afternoon, a bunch of us were caught by the river's current, and we began to struggle back upstream attempting to reach the sandbar where we started. I looked up and wondered if those were the last clouds I would ever see. A man I do not know and can never thank, yelled, "Swim with the current!"

I turned around and shortly afterward reached for the oar he held out to me. God used him to save my life, but only if I would receive his comment, turn, and reach for the oar.

Although I don't know the man who yelled "swim with the current," I now recognize that he was just one of an unnumbered multitude who sacrificed and gave to me all those young years: teachers, coaches, preachers, Scout leaders, Boys' State sponsors, relatives, friends, and unknown people who bought the magazines and Christmas wreaths we sold from door to door, and paid us to mow their lawns. Men and women who built our houses and our schools, kept us safe on the streets, and made this nation operate. All I had to do was to open my eyes, my ears, and my hands and receive.

Later, I realized that my youthful swimming experience contained a much deeper lesson. God has a plan for each individual life and for history. I can go through life trying to go my way—or I can submit to Him and let Him use me to carry out His plan for my life.

A little poem says it well:

> *God knows where we're going,*
> *And God knows where we've been.*
> *God has made eternal plans for us*
> *That will never end.*
>
> *History's on a countdown,*
> *It isn't just a whim;*
> *For God knows where we're going,*
> *And God knows where we've been.*

We can spend our years fighting the current, which will wear us out and take us backward faster than we can go forward. Or we can turn around and use the current (like wind in the sails of a ship) to go the way God has planned for us. Since His will is ultimately going to control, and He wants far more goodness for us than we could ever imagine, it only makes sense to go His way.

Many years later, I made that decision and began to "swim with the current." I never regretted it.

1940s *The Gifts of Manhood and Marriage*

World War II dominated the 1940s. I entered the old Army Air Corps (later renamed the US Air Force) in 1943 at age 18. The day the war ended in August, 1945, I was out over the Pacific in a B-29 returning from the last mission of the war. I was 20 years and 4 days old and unharmed. Those years helped to give me my manhood, if I was willing to receive it and to use it. Many were injured or lost their lives, including my brother, Leon Martin, who was killed in a B-24 air crash over England in March 1945. He left behind a wife, a small daughter, and an unborn daughter who arrived a few months after his death. He and thousands of others sacrificed everything so we could have a free America in a freer world.

Over fifty years later, I read a new book entitled, *The Last Mission*, by Jim Smith and Malcolm McConnell. It advanced the theory that our flight unknowingly stopped a coup by some of the Japanese military, who were attempting to capture the Imperial Palace and the Emperor and keep the war going. When our planes went by Tokyo, the Japanese government "blacked out" the city and the Emperor's palace, and apparently thwarted the rebels' plans. This all showed me that God might be doing something through us of which we are not aware. In our case, it arguably meant saving thousands of military and civilians from being killed if the war had continued. We need to plan and act, but the final results are still in God's hands. As Proverbs 16:9 says:

In his heart a man plans his course,
but the Lord determines his steps.

In 1946 I returned to Kansas University where I met Ellie. We were married in 1948, and she helped keep me afloat during Law School, and for the next 59 years. She has given me more and taught me more than any other person, including how to be a better receiver. No matter what you give her—a thought, a comment, a home, a flower—she loves receiving, and she brightens your heart when you give to her. She even listens and actually wants to receive what others have to say! She has loved me enough to risk irritating me to help me do better. She also taught me simplicity. Before an early trial, I tried out my argument on her. She listened and said, "Why don't you say this and this and this?"

I was offended, and didn't want to receive her advice, so I said, "I just did say that." She responded stoutly, "Then say it so I can understand it!"

This time I received it.

The Bible says,

> *...what God has joined together, let man not separate.*
> (Matthew 19:6b)

We do not "become one" by our efforts after we marry; instead we receive "oneness" from God when we marry. *Our job is to hold on to His gift of oneness and not lose it or destroy it!*

One important way we do that is to listen and learn from our spouses.

1950s *The Gifts of Work and Family*

The 1950s was the decade of the Korean War, the Cold War, the birth control pill, and mass television. My law practice began early in 1951 in an office building that had operators for the elevators and spittoons in the halls. Getting to do the work we want to do with people we enjoy is one of God's great gifts (Ecclesiastes 3:13). Now I realize how much I have received, free of charge, from my partners and other lawyers, clients, office staffs, the legal system, and the entire work world.

Let me tell you one early event my first major client loved to relate. My young friend was taking responsibility for their family business and wanted to build his own team. I will never forget the day he brought his father to discuss our representation of their company. What must that older man have thought as he entered my small office, with a used desk and two straight-back chairs! Here he was talking with a young, relatively inexperienced lawyer about to be entrusted with legal responsibility for the company he had been building for many years. As expected, my friend indicated he wanted to use our newly formed two-man firm. His father's reply was a classic: "That's all right, Son. But what will we do if we have a *problem?*"

Fortunately, our relationship lasted over forty years. And the event taught me the valuable lesson of having faith in the next generation.

As our law firm began to grow, so did our young family. In our generation, larger families were more common. We rejoiced every time God blessed us by allowing us to receive a new life into our fold. First, He gave us five children and a nephew to live with us. They in turn had fifteen children, and now we are starting to reap the harvest of great-grandchildren. All have been great blessings and given us far more love, joy, and pleasure than we ever knew was possible. An unexpected bonus for us has been watching them receive and then enjoy, increase, and distribute God's gifts to those who follow them.

On our bedroom wall hangs a needlepoint given to Ellie by a dear friend, quoting from the Apostle John, who wrote,

> *I have no greater joy than to hear that*
> *my children are walking in the truth.*
> (3 John 1:4)

I believe John was referring to children in the faith. So we rejoice when every child of God, whether born to us or simply entrusted to us for a period of time, walks with Him.

Our prayer for each child is not that they would have worldly success, but rather that they would follow, love, obey, walk with, and serve the Lord. When they do, we are comfortable that He will take care of all their needs. As they have grown into maturity, we find them increasingly giving us counsel and help. And strangely enough, the older we get, the more we want to receive it.

1960s *The Gift of Faith*

The 1960s saw a nation divided over a war in Vietnam and a war on values at home. As I approached the last of this decade, I sensed that my spiritual journey was reaching a turning point. I had seen "full-time, professional" Christians who were expected to be "holy," but for the rest of us, our work worlds seemed to operate on the hard realities of life that might or might not conform to scriptural principles. Gradually, my quest took me into books that I discovered had been written by others whose search paralleled my own. I finally realized that I was on the threshold of the eternal question that all of us must ultimately face:

"What is the real purpose of life—and death?"

For years I wrestled with God. Gradually I began to see, especially through the writings of certain authors, that it was a test of the will. Either God's will or my will was going to rule my life—and it had to be total, unconditional surrender!

One reason I believe it is so hard for some of us, particularly men, to accept Christ is that we have to humble ourselves and receive, rather than earn, eternal life. As the Apostle John writes:

> *He came to that which was his own,*
> *but his own did not **receive** him.*
> *Yet to all who **received** him,*
> *to those who believed in his name,*
> *he gave the right to become children of God—*
> (John 1:11–12, emphasis added)

Finally, in true labor lawyer style, I negotiated a settlement with God. I couldn't bring myself to surrender my will in one step, but I agreed in the early summer of 1969 that I would surrender on August 10, my 44th birthday. The birthday finally arrived. Following a celebration with our family, and without advising anyone of my intentions, I walked up the stairway, down the hallway, and into our bedroom. There I knelt alone and confessed something like this:

> "Lord, I commit all of myself to you that I am able;
> and I accept Jesus as your divine Son."

That was over thirtyeight years ago, and I have never regretted my decision. There have been good times and hard times, but my life since then has had more peace and fulfillment than I ever realized was possible. The Bible tells us we don't earn faith; it is a free gift. Ephesians 2:8–9 says it this way:

> *For it is by grace you have been saved, through faith—*
> *And this not from yourselves, it is the gift of God—*
> *not by works, so that no one can boast.*

But we do have to humble ourselves and receive!

The Bible itself is one of the greatest free gifts of all time, if we will receive it. Dozens of people over hundreds of years wrote these words from God and offered them totally without charge. No copyrights, no fees, just a free gift. And with it God also offers the marvelous gift of forgiveness, if I am willing to confess, receive forgiveness, and forgive others (1 John 1:9; Matthew 6:12–15).

1970s *The Gift of Relationships*

The 1970s saw a presidency crumble over Watergate and a nation caught in runaway inflation. On August 10, 1974, our family was seated around the table after completing a birthday dinner, and I was feeling philosophical. I said:

> "Some time ago I heard of a man who was discussing the stages of life. He said that when he was a young boy, his greatest desire was for food. As he grew older, his desire changed to money, because that would allow him to buy all the food or other things he wanted. Still later, his desire was for time, because he found that with time he could make the money to buy the things he wanted. But finally, he concluded that the most important thing in life was relationships. That is where I am now."

Then I announced as I surveyed all those nearest and dearest to me:

> "To me, relationships—you all—
> are the most important thing in life!"

There was quiet for a moment. Then our 19-year-old son, with a smile in his eyes, spoke up and said,

> "Can I have your money?"

Earlier in my life, relationships had not been so important to me. Much of the time I had found myself living in labor law conflicts. At one point we had our own office bombed. Now, in my 40s and

50s, I was beginning to experience one of the most rewarding blessings of my new life in Christ, as I gradually moved from an adversarial climate into a world with less discord and more harmony. Not perfect, of course, but much more enjoyable than the environment I had previously known.

I had begun reading the Bible regularly, not just for study but because I was desperate for guidance about how to live my life with others. As I read, I saw that God has given us roles in the various institutions in which He has placed us. When I was willing to receive and act on my role as a man, husband, father, employer, citizen, etc., and carry out the Biblical responsibilities of each role, and then help others find and carry out their biblical roles, I found harmony rather than discord in more and more of my relationships.

I also discovered that relationships with relatives and friends and acquaintances became much deeper and more meaningful when we became brothers and sisters in Christ.

I encourage you that we can have more harmony in all our institutions, which will bless us and those around us, if we follow Jesus and His Word rather than the ever-changing precepts of the world. But we must be willing to receive what the Bible tells us, and carry out our roles in each area of life.

From all this, I also learned another valuable lesson: If we keep our relationships, we will seldom if ever have litigation. What a great world that would be!

1980s *The Gift of Discipleship*

The 1980s saw the Berlin Wall come down and the Cold War end, as the Russian empire splintered. During these years, we also watched a watershed of history as we moved steadily from an industrial to an informational world.

At the heart of Jesus' ministry 2000 years ago was His command to His followers to

> *...go and make disciples...*
> (Matthew 28:19)

As I look back, I realize how much I have received from a few modern-day followers of Jesus, who carried out that command and discipled me in the years after my decision to follow Him. No one ever charged me. They simply held out their hand, gave me what they had, and helped me grow closer to what God had planned for me to be and to do. All I had to do was to receive. Sometimes the process was exciting, sometimes it was hard, and sometimes it was humbling. Let me give you one example.

Several of us were invited to go as a group of laymen to Billings, Montana, to share our faith in that community. On the evening before a breakfast meeting, I was asked if I would tell about my spiritual journey the next morning. My prayer that night was modeled after John the Baptist, who said,

> *He must become greater; I must become less.*
> (John 3:30)

Little did I know what I was praying!

The following morning, when we arrived in the large banquet room in the hotel, we saw that the stage had been raised several feet above the floor, and there were rough wooden steps leading up to the speakers' platform. When I started up the stairs, one foot slipped, I fell spread-eagle across the stage, and an embarrassed hush descended on the room. As I picked myself up and moved to the microphone, all I could think of was a jumbled version of some words by the Apostle Peter, so I looked out over the audience and said:

"Humble yourself under the mighty hand of God!"

Laughter broke the tension, God was glorified, and I survived.

The early Apostles were described in the Bible as "fools for Christ" (1 Corinthians 4:10). Sometimes we do the most to advance God's Kingdom when we appear the most foolish in the eyes of the world. Jesus said:

> *Whoever believes in me, as the Scripture has said,*
> *streams of living water shall flow from within him.*
> (John 7:38)

God meant for us to act as rivers carrying out into the world what He entrusts to us, although it may be embarrassing or even dangerous. If we keep His gifts to ourselves, we become a Dead Sea: stagnant, stale, and smelly. And someday we will be called to account!

1990s *The Gift of Love*

The 1990s opened with a short, successful Gulf War and ended with an embarrassed presidency and a tech stock bubble. In 1990, I was nearing my 65th birthday and thinking about retirement and what I was to do with the rest of my life. On May 7, I was awakened by a clear voice saying:

> "Your assignment for the rest of your life
> is simply to love people and to love me."

When Jesus was asked, "Teacher, which is the greatest commandment *in the Law?*" he replied:

> *Love the Lord your God with all your heart and with all your soul and*
> *with all your mind.*
> *This is the first and greatest commandment.*
> *And the second is like it:*
> *"Love your neighbor as yourself."*
> *All the **Law and the Prophets***
> *hang on these two commandments.*
> (Matthew 22:36–40, emphasis added)

Later, Jesus gave a *new* command about love when He was preparing to leave this earth:

> *A **new** command I give you: Love one another.*
> ***As I have loved you**, so you must love one another.*
> (John 13:34, emphasis added)

By these few words, Jesus changed the standard from loving as *we* want to be loved, to loving as *He* has loved *us!* What a giant leap! It moved from *contractual* love to *sacrificial* love.

As the Apostle John explained

> *This is how we know what love is:*
> *Jesus Christ laid down His life for us.*
> *And we ought to lay down our lives for our brothers.*
> (1 John 3:16)

If this is to be our challenge, we need to ask ourselves:

"Why would I lay down my life for others?"

I believe the answer is gratitude. To me, gratitude for what I have received (or will receive) from God is the most powerful and satisfying motivation there is. When my motivation comes from gratitude for God's love and grace, rather than working to get a reward, it makes God and others the focal point of my life. It brings humility instead of pride. And it makes me want to give thanks for receiving an inheritance I cannot earn instead of claiming a reward for my efforts here on earth. When my sense of worth comes because God loves me as His child and not because of my good works, I never lose my self-esteem whether or not I perform well in this world. And my reason for living continues as long as God has me living, since He can use me as a receiver even when I can no longer be a giver.

Most of us have heard the familiar verse:

It is more blessed to give than receive.
(Acts 20:35b)

But the Bible also reminds us:

We love because he (God) *first loved us.*
(1 John 4:19)

In other words, we have to *receive* love before we have any love to give to others. So now I want to open my heart and receive love from the Lord and all the people He brings into my life—for only then can I carry out my assignment to "love people and love God" for the rest of my life.

2000 *The Gift of Growing Older*

It seemed almost poetic to close the old century and millennium and move into the first decade of an exciting new 21st century at the same time I began moving into my own closing years and looking more earnestly upward toward Heaven. Ecclesiastes 3 says there is "a time to be born and time to die." But it also says God "made everything beautiful in its time." That has to include old age. *If we don't want to grow older, we must think this world is better than Heaven, since old age, for most of us, is the gateway!*

When we are young, we look forward to growing older. Most teenagers can't wait to reach age 16 so they can get a driver's license. Young people in the work force often wish they could be a little older and more experienced to further their careers. But at about age 40, we begin to see the end of the road more clearly, and many of us fear growing older. I believe the key is not to fear, nor to fight, growing older, but simply to accept it as a natural and necessary part of our life journey. As one woman said, rather contentedly, "I fought turning 40. I embraced turning 50!"

Although we start life as receivers, once we have known the thrill, and sometimes the power, of being in charge, it often becomes very difficult to embrace growing older. We dread being humbled and increasingly forced to be dependent and receive from others, like a little child.

But receiving is part of what makes life have value. If we ever eliminate all the poor, sick, elderly, and needy, we will eliminate love from the world, *because every act of love requires a lovee as well as a lover!* We each must play our part, sometimes as givers and sometimes as receivers. And there are times receiving may be the most important!

Ellie and I are now living in a retirement center, which incidentally is a great place to learn a lot about gracious receiving. Paradoxically, we repeatedly say this is one of the best times of our lives. We are not so bothered by the big things the world thinks are important, and we can concentrate on the things that God says are eternal:

God, His Love, His Word, and People!

Conclusion

Now it's time to close. Thanks for letting me share these moments with you. It has been a rare privilege to reflect on life and pass on to you some of what God has given me. As I look back at these eighty-plus years, I am drawn again to the title of the book I refused to let my friend buy for me so many years ago: *Let God Love You!* That one thought seems to be the starting point—and now the ending point of all of life.

When we *"Let God Love Us"*, His gifts flow into us and grow until they naturally overflow out onto everything and everyone around us. We do become salt and light to our world. The initial issue is not what we do for God or for others, but what God does through us. It all starts with humbling ourselves to receive, so we will have something to enjoy and to give.

My generation's time is now coming to a conclusion. I have read that more than three-fourths of all those who served in World War II are gone, and the rest of us are dying at a rate of over 1000 a day. As the end draws near, I sense an increasing urgency to tell others about the greatest of all God's gifts—"eternal life in Christ Jesus" (Romans 6:23; I Corinthians 15:3–4).

For the last 2000 years, the good news of this eternal gift has been faithfully passed from one generation to the next. Now it has reached our time in history. Once we receive the gift, it becomes our privilege to pass it on to those who are following.

My closing prayer, therefore, is that all who hear God's call will surrender and follow Him. Then we can look forward to receiving one final gift that is the best of all: spending eternity in the Kingdom of God, with Him and His Family!

See you in Heaven!

Part VI

For Such A Time As This!

And who knows but that you have come to royal position
for such a time as this?
(Esther 4:14b)

Preface

2009

In 1969 I bowed my knees and committed my life to Jesus. I was deeply concerned, of course, that clients wanted a tough, no-holds-barred attorney and I would lose business if people found out I was a true follower of Christ. Finally, my wife and I went to Colorado for a week so I could meditate and think through the problem.

One afternoon on a hillside near Gunnison, Colorado, God gave me the answer. It came from the biblical story of Esther as she struggled with whether or not to reveal her Jewish identity to her pagan husband, the king, and ask him to save her people from being slaughtered.

When I read her courageous example, I decided it was time for me, too, to take a stand. So I dedicated my law practice to God and said, like Esther,

> *And if I perish, I perish.*
> (Esther 4:16b)

The question that challenged Esther (and later me) came from her relative, Mordecai, who confronted her with the reason for her existence, and has become a symbol of God's providential control of history:

> *And who knows but that you have come to royal position*
> *for such a time as this?*
> (Esther 4:15)

As the years have gone by, I have become disturbingly aware that God's hand in history is becoming increasingly evident. During the events described in the Bible, there were often long periods of dormancy, such as the 400 years of Egyptian captivity and the 400 years between the Old and New Testaments. In each case, these were followed by a great outpouring of God's visible hand. It seems we are now facing another one of those times as we enter into this third millennium since Christ first walked on earth. Because the Bible says a "thousand years...are like a day," it has even made me wonder if it could possibly be that AD 2000 could be the dawning of another "third day" following Jesus' resurrection and promised return.

I suppose that is too much to expect, but because of the momentous times I sense are facing us and the world, it seems that Mordecai's challenging words, "For Such A Time As This," are an appropriate title for our discussion.

Remember, of course, that we all err. So test what I say, hold on to that which is good (of God)—and discard the rest.

From Grandpa With Love

For Such A Time As This!

In 1999, I wrote *Four Generations: A Journey Through Life,* to pass on to our family and others some of my thoughts about the first 75 years of life. After reviewing history, I reached the following conclusions about the approaching new century:

"Interestingly, history (His Story as recorded in the Bible and the church) seems to follow a rather methodical pattern, like many of our lives, and to be marked by a similar roller coaster of ups and downs, peaks and valleys. I believe it looks like this."

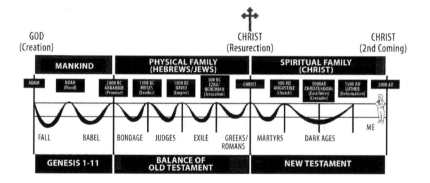

It is difficult to see either a monumental peak or valley since the Reformation in AD 1500. But if we continue these 500-year cycles, it seems likely we are on the threshold of a *very* historic time around the year AD 2000. Many seem to have a sense of anticipation, or foreboding, almost as if we were feeling the birth pangs of an event about to occur. The end of the Cold War, the fragmentation of historic institutions, and the explosion of technology have left us unsettled. For the first time in history, computer networking, globalization, and the intertwining of economies all seem to point to the possibility of a new one-world era.

For those who are drawn to eschatology, this may herald the "end times" spoken of so graphically by Daniel (in the Book of Daniel) and by Jesus (e.g., Matthew 24). For others, such a series of events point to unlimited new opportunities. And for still others, it portends terrible chaos and difficulties as we go through the coming years.

I am not a prophet. But I sense we are moving into a time of political, economic, and social change greater than we have seen for 500 years—perhaps greater than we have ever known. *Therefore, I believe we need to be prepared spiritually and physically! To me this means being sure we are fully surrendered and ready to meet Him whether He comes here or calls us Home; and also being ready to weather any storms and to help others spiritually and physically if chaotic times do occur during our lifetime."*

2009 (A Look Around)

Now it is 2009—and the changes have come much more quickly and were far deeper and more dramatic than I could have imagined. Within three years, the tech stock market bubble had burst; Islamic militants had successfully attacked the World Trade Center in New York, and the Pentagon in Washington, DC; and our nation was at war against terrorism in Afghanistan and Iraq. In addition, the culture war over social values, particularly those involving homosexuality and marriage, was sharply dividing our nation, as the US Supreme Court outlawed state sodomy laws, and states began approving same-sex marriage.

As the decade proceeded, we continued to experience one numbing event after another. National debt levels grew astronomically as we borrowed money to fund wars abroad and domestic programs such as Medicare Prescription Drug Coverage for seniors, as well as Federal money for education. The economic roller coaster of fast money accelerated after the Federal Government naively opened the home market to those who were unable to afford them, and greedy speculators seized the opportunity to leverage the monies entrusted to them. The result was a huge increase in housing, combined with skyrocketing prices and sub-prime mortgages, followed by the collapse of that market, and culminating in the worst housing and stock market corrections since the Great Depression of the 1930s.

In just ten short years, these events—combined with our changing technical, ethnic, and cultural climate—have resulted in the election of a virtually unknown to the Presidency; added trillions of dollars to our national debt; brought Government intervention in the business world in a way that has critics speaking of socialism and fascism reminiscent of Europe and other nations; flooded our nation with illegal immigration, spurred on by unscrupulous employers looking for cheap labor and only tepidly controlled by political groups seeking converts to their party rolls; and increased crime and a murderous border war among drug cartels seeking to control the flow of illegal drugs into our nation.

1945–2009 (A Look Back)

World War II ended in 1945. As a victor, the United States helped bring peaceful new governments to stabilize former enemy nations and then helped the world regain its political and economic well-being by encouraging and housing the United Nations in New York, and by advancing gifts, loans, and other help around the world.

The 20th century and the early part of the 21st century have been the era of the American Empire. But it has been an Empire dedicated not to conquest and increased territory but rather to peace and the spread of representative democracy throughout the world. We have fought wars in Korea, Vietnam, Granada, Panama, Kosovo, Iraq, and Afghanistan, and had innumerable skirmishes around the globe. Today, we have military outposts throughout the world, all dedicated to a desire for peace, not conquest. We have basically acted as the peacekeeper of the world for over half a century.

But these efforts have cost us dearly in manpower and money. We have spent vast sums we did not have. In essence, we have borrowed to spend—both at home and abroad. The prosperity we have so loudly acclaimed during our generation has been not only from our productive efforts, but has also included destroying the value of our money by inflation (both intentionally and unintentionally) and by borrowing from citizens and foreign groups, and we now find ourselves deeply in debt. In hindsight it seems we have been supported by a national program similar to a reverse mortgage, which gradually uses up the value of an aging person's home.

In some ways the United States has been to the 20th century and early 21st century what Great Britain was to the 19th and early

20th century, when it was said, "The sun never sets on the British Empire." At the close of World War II in 1945, Britain controlled vast areas of the world, including India, large portions of Africa (including the Suez Canal in Egypt), West Indies Islands, and territories in Asia and the Pacific. In just 40 short years, she lost virtually all of them. By 1985, Great Britain's empire status was over.

The United States now stands at the helm of the world. But it appears our time as the world leader is also drawing to a close. Perhaps we are where Britain was at the close of World War II. If so, the next 40 years will probably mark a great change for us— as we, like every older person, moves on and new generations succeed us. This is only natural. Nothing lasts forever. Nations are mortal, so they die, just as every person and institution in the world ultimately must do.

The aging of our nation is evident. We are no longer principally known as producers; instead we are now known as consumers. We are no longer creditors; we are the world's largest debtor nation. Our own Government borrows trillions of dollars and gives or loans them as stimulus to prime the pump and encourage us to continue our credit binge by borrowing to buy! We no longer expand by our own birth rate but through massive legal and illegal immigration.

It appears we, as a nation, have become much like a retiree who comes to the older years and wants to live the easy life. Apparently a majority of our people and our elected representatives no longer have the will or the resources to be the benevolent uncrowned leader of the world.

When I reached my 80s, I told our children in essence, "I am no longer in charge. I know you already knew that, but I wanted to make it official!"

In much the same way, it looks as if those currently in power are announcing to the world our nation's retirement as the leader, peacekeeper, and economic engine of the world.

2009 (A Look At The Future)

In earlier years we were an isolationist nation. We were told by our first President, George Washington, to stay out of foreign entanglements. Just before the dawn of the 20th century, we stepped into the International scene through the Spanish-American War. Throughout the 20th century, we increasingly moved into such entanglements. By the close of World War II in 1945, we had become a superpower capable of keeping peace and encouraging prosperity throughout the world. We have played this role for the past 60-plus years.

A Changed People

But now we are a different people. The years have seen a change in our ethnic, religious, political, and economic models. The mood of our population has gradually moved from self-sufficiency and leadership of the world, to a homogenized society increasingly dependent on giant corporations and government at all levels for our jobs, our decisions, our pay, our health, and our morals.

Moving Toward Globalization

This new reality has recently been symbolized by our new President and other political and economic leaders, displaying a willingness (and sometimes an eagerness) to submit our nation as merely one of many who will make global policy and laws—that will result in giving up our national sovereignty, piece by piece, through treaties and various international agreements and tribunals. Many in positions of economic and political power increasingly see themselves as citizens of the world rather than simply being citizens of one nation known as the United States of America.

These events have produced mounting cries for globalization and a new world order to control global warming, global credit crises, global crimes, global wars, and other global problems. In some ways we seem to be repeating, globally, what we have largely achieved, nationally, i.e., just as State Sovereignty has largely been preempted by Federal Supremacy, so are we now moving toward preempting National Sovereignty in favor of Global Supremacy.

It seems inevitable that global government will, of necessity, follow global information (on the Internet), global banking (and possibly a new one-world currency), global commerce (including multinational corporations larger than many nations), global environmental concerns, global travel, and the desire for global peace. But it probably will not come easily or quickly. Just as our nation's move to local, then state, and finally Federal Government supremacy took many years and much conflict, so will it probably take a great deal of time and conflict to consolidate the world. But it appears it is going to happen. The generations who are following us need to recognize it and decide how they are going to deal with it.

At the recent G20 Economic Summit, England's Prime Minister Gordon Brown summarized it this way:

"The old Washington consensus is over...
a new consensus," based on "taking global action together...
A *new world order* is emerging."
(Wichita Eagle, April 3, 2009; emphasis added)

Filling The Vacuum
Our President now travels the world, confessing our national arrogance and promising a new era of reconciliation. While this will no doubt give us a temporary reprieve and enhance our popularity with others around the globe, it ignores the much more serious, although subtle problem:

**Who will step in to fill the vacuum that will now occur
as we leave the throne?**

For centuries Rome kept peace around the known world. *Pax Romana* (Roman peace) came to symbolize the order this superpower brought to the world. But when Rome fell, civilization fell with it—for a thousand years we have come to know as the Dark Ages.

We are leaving the throne voluntarily, rather than by force. Hopefully, it will not be a repeat of that dark time. But history tells us that even when the King dies peacefully, there is often a blood bath as the next generation struggles for power. I am concerned that there may be an arms race and the possibility of widespread war, famine, and pestilence during the coming years, as others (e.g., China, Russia, Iran, North Korea, Militant Islamists, etc.) seek to become the superpower or powers of the 21st century, while the world moves toward Global Government.

Scattering and Gathering
Ecclesiastes 3:1, 5 says,

> *There is a time for everything...a time to scatter...*
> *and a time to gather.*

It is much like breathing that keeps us alive: we breathe in, and then we breathe out.

As I read these verses, I was puzzled why scattering came before gathering, until I realized that God first scattered on the earth as He breathed life into His creation. After that He gave His command for us to repeat this process as we "fill the earth and subdue it" (Genesis 1:28).

This same pattern has continued all through history as a husband and wife "gather" a family together, then "scatter" them so they can repeat the process. And so it is in all of life, as everything is born, carries out its purpose in life, and then dies. Jesus gave this example in John 12:24:

> *I tell you the truth, unless a kernel of wheat*
> *falls to the ground and dies,*
> *it remains only a single seed.*
> *But if it dies, it produces many seeds.*

It seems God does want us to build and increase—however, it is not to make ourselves bigger and more powerful, but that we may scatter it all in God's name, and for His glory!

Unfortunately, we seem to like to *gather* more than *scatter!* Mankind's rebellious nature quickly became evident as they built the Tower of Babel, reflected in Genesis 11:1–9, which says,

> *Come, let us build ourselves a city,*
> *with a tower that reaches to the heavens,*
> *so that we may make a name for ourselves and **not be scattered***
> *over the face of the whole earth."*
> (Emphasis added)

But God would not allow them to wrest control from Him,

> *So the Lord **scattered** them from there over all the earth,*
> *and they stopped building the city.*
> (Emphasis added)

Jesus gave similar instructions at the beginning of the New Testament when He told His disciples, as recorded in Acts 1:8,

> *...you will be my witnesses in Jerusalem,*
> *and in all Judea and Samaria,*
> *and to the **ends of the earth**.*
> (Emphasis added)

But Christianity didn't begin to explode across the world until Acts 8:1, when...

> *a great persecution broke out against the church at Jerusalem,*
> *and all except the apostles were **scattered***
> *throughout Judea and Samaria.*
> (Emphasis added)

God's unwavering call throughout history has been for mankind to *scatter* after we *gather.* Yet every generation, including ours and those who will follow us, attempts to build its own Tower of Babel. We have always failed—and we will always fail! *Because God will not yield His Power and Glory to us!*

Our current culture seeks ever-bigger companies, governments, programs, and charitable organizations, and looks for great leaders (some of whom receive millions of dollars for their efforts) to show us the way—and the effect is often to paralyze us from being individuals who do what God has created us to be and to do.

We are often encouraged to organize and bring all our combined force and might against our adversaries. We become uniform, a regular army. We rely on a leader to guide, direct, and then control us. We are not free to move except as we are told and in the way we are told. We submit ourselves to worldly institutions, hoping and sometimes believing that they can accomplish what we want and bring a utopia here on earth. We are told that if the right people can just get in control of the government or the company or the group, our belief system will prevail.

We may bring a change in our culture by force, but submission by worldly force is not what God is seeking in His Kingdom. He wants us to come into His Family and Kingdom voluntarily—and then scatter His love and His message of grace and hope to the world.

Again, I want to emphasize that I am not a prophet. But history tells us this basic scenario has played out innumerable times over the centuries, and reality tells us to be aware it can happen again. So here are two questions to ask ourselves. The first is this:

"Am I Willing to Watch and Trust God as He Moves Forward at 'Such a Time as This'?"

The answer for me is the same as it was ten years ago in *Four Generations*:

"As we view the broad historical picture of what God has done over the centuries, and what He may be about to do now, it makes us realize just how small we are in God's total plan. Each of us *is* important and significant to God (e.g., Psalm 8:4–8). But when we finally see ourselves in relation to Him, we must conclude, like Job:

Surely I spoke of things I did not understand,
things too wonderful for me to know…My ears had heard of you,
but now my eyes have seen you. Therefore, I despise myself
and repent in dust and ashes.
(Job 42:3b, 5–6)

As we increasingly see the magnitude of God's plan, we no longer strive to hold so tightly to our own power and possessions, and our few years in history. Maturity seems to bring with it a willingness to let God have His way. Instead of wanting an epitaph centered on us, mature believers often look for ways for God to receive the glory and recognition. Many are not only willing but increasingly desire that Jesus might increase and they might decrease.

Life is not a meaningless circle. God created us and despite our rebellion He is calling each generation to return and enjoy Him throughout our lives and into all eternity. I believe a little poem summarizes it well:

> *God knows where we're going,*
> *And God knows where we've been;*
> *God has made eternal plans for us,*
> *That will never end.*

> *History's on a countdown,*
> *It isn't just a whim;*
> *For God knows where we're going,*
> *And God knows where we've been.*

The Bible makes it clear that God has a plan for all creation, and that includes a plan for each of us. As He says in Jeremiah 29:11:

> *"For I know the plans I have for you," declares the Lord,*
> *"plans to prosper you and not to harm you,*
> *plans to give you hope and a future."*

As a result, we can now begin to relax and watch with interest and even some contentment to see what God intends to do through this last generation of our lives."

This brings us to the second, and often more perplexing, question:

"What Am I to Do During 'Such a Time as This'?"

A short time ago a man said to me after we talked about some of the challenges we have been discussing,

> "You have posed great challenges which lie ahead.
> My question is 'What are we supposed to do about them?'"

It brought to mind a similar question I asked an older mentor many years ago while we were spending a day together. He did not answer at first; later he looked at me and answered forcefully,

> "Do that which you believe to be most important!"

Through the years I have heard similar answers voiced by others. I was sitting in a small meeting of believers with a guest speaker. When asked how we know what God wants us to do, he said,

> "I think if God were sitting next to me now
> and I asked that question,
> He would answer, 'What do you want to do?'"

A seasoned veteran missionary turned politician in essence said it this way to a group of us who had gathered to hear his thoughts:

> "I decided to try and meet the greatest need. But later," he said,
> "I realized I couldn't always meet that need.
> So I amended my goal to the greatest need I can help meet."

Lorne Sanny, former head of the Navigator Ministry, gave a simple, but powerful, talk that, as I remember, encouraged believers to...

"Do what you can, where you are, with what you have"

based on the story of Shamgar (Judges 3:31) who "struck down six hundred Philistines with an ox goad."

And many have said simply,

"Bloom where you are planted."

All of them were saying in different ways that God will direct each of us in the way we should go—if we are constantly in touch with Him. And what He tells *me* is not necessarily what He will tell *you*. He answers each of us according to our unique circumstances.

It has been excellent advice.

Conclusion

Realism is not always pleasant. Jeremiah was thought a traitor because he announced, as recorded in the book of Jeremiah, that Judah was going to fall and be conquered by the Babylonians. He was a realist, not a pessimist. In fact, he was such an optimist that he bought land and had the deed preserved so his heirs would have the property when they returned from captivity seventy years later.

In the meantime, he made it clear that God has a plan for all creation, by leaving us the great message of hope set forth in Jeremiah 29:11 that we quoted above:

> *"For I know the plans I have for you," declares the Lord,*
> *"plans to prosper you and not to harm you,*
> *plans to give you hope and a future."*

Although Jeremiah was right about the demise of his country, he wasn't pleased by what happened. In fact he was so overcome with sorrow over the fall of his beloved Jerusalem that he became known as the weeping prophet, and wrote the great lament we know as the book of Lamentations.

We, too, are not always pleased by the way history unfolds. But we deny reality at our peril. The world has been trying for centuries to build a new world, but each time it fails because man has a fatal flaw.

We are tempted to join the effort and try and perfect the world. But the Bible reminds us that as believers we are "aliens and strangers in the world" (1 Peter 2:11). Our job is not to make everything work out right—*our job is to show the world an alternative (Jesus Christ), Who is going to get it right.* In the meantime, we are to "believe" (John 6:29) and follow the description of David, who "served God's purpose in his own generation" (Acts 13:36a).

Whether we work individually or in government, corporations, or other organizations, and whether we become rich and famous or live modestly and unknown is not the real issue. The real issue is whether we are serving the Kingdom of the World or the Kingdom of God.

God will take care of His Story (History). Our job is to serve Him while He does it. When our time here is over, we can live together with Him and all His Family in the perfect world He will bring to replace this old worn-out one, when its time is over.

We don't need to wait for someone to form a committee or an organization, or find a leader to use what God has given each of us, *"For Such A Time As This."* We simply need to get started and then continue what He gives us to be and do, until He calls us Home.

I look forward to seeing you there—for eternity!

From Grandpa With Love

Part VII

am I—?

God said to Moses, ***"I AM WHO I AM."***
(Exodus 3:14, emphasis added)

Preface

2010

God referred to Himself as *"I AM"* (which we often translate as "the Lord") when he appeared to Moses in Exodus 3. When Jesus began His ministry hundreds of years later, He, too, referred to Himself as "I am." For example, "I am the bread of life" in John 6:35; "I am the light of the world" in John 8:12; and most dramatically, when he announced, "I tell you the truth...before Abraham was born, I am!" in John 8:58.

It is *"I AM"* who declares the truth throughout the Bible. Since we humans are not "the Lord," we can only seek God's truth, attempt to apply it in our own lives, and pass it on to others.

The title of this booklet is *"am I—?"* It is purposely spelled with a small *a* and purposely drafted as a question. Hopefully, this will emphasize that what you are about to read on the following pages are merely some of my questions, together with some thoughts and possible solutions as they have appeared to me.

The questions arose over the years as I became increasingly intrigued by words or phrases that are often used (and sometimes misused) in tandem. Some, such as *Old and Young*, were opposites. Others, such as *Jealousy and Envy*, were close companions. But repeatedly they were discussed together.

I discovered that I often did not know the correct definitions for the terms, nor the real relationship between each pair. This started me on a search. What were the meanings of the words, and why did they have an almost magnetic power to stay glued together in our minds and in our speech?

I concluded these twin terms often represent some of our difficult dilemmas in life. Some (e.g., *Wise and Foolish*) were like non-identical twins, bracketing opposite ends of a concept. Others (e.g., *Teaching and Preaching*) appeared to be more like identical twins who, although never completely the same, were so similar that we need both of them to reveal all we want to express. It became evident that each of these twin words or phrases provided a concise form to express a truth and be memorable enough to remember. In a way, they were similar to the comparisons found in the proverbs used in the Bible and other literature.

Because these twins (and occasional triplets) have been helpful to me, I decided to pass them on. Some of these are discussed in more detail in other writings but repeated here, hoping the shorter, concise approach will provide a fresh insight into some eternal truths.

The brevity is both a strength and a weakness. The thoughts are easier to digest but more easily misunderstood, especially since we all come with different backgrounds and assumptions.

Be assured my goal is not to tell you what you must believe, but simply to express what God has given me, and encourage you to think and pray and reach decisions as the Holy Spirit leads you.

The concepts are not in any particular order since they cover such a wide spectrum of life. There are thirty-one questions, so they can be read as short, daily meditations over a month, following the pattern many have used for the thirty-one chapters in the book of Proverbs. Others may prefer them for a Bible Study.

But, remember, we all err. So, as you read and meditate on these thoughts, hold on to what is good (of God)—and discard the rest.

From Grandpa With Love

One

am I Judging or Discerning?

Judging others occurs when I decide
what should happen to you
because of what you did.

Discerning occurs when I decide
what would happen to me
if I did what you did.

Only authorities are to judge others.
All wise people are to discern.
(Matthew 7:1–6; 1 Corinthians 6:1–5)

Why do you look at the
speck of sawdust in your brother's eye
and pay no attention to the plank
in your own eye?
(Matthew 7:3)

Two

am I Leading or Commanding?

Leaders are so attractive
that others follow because they want to.

Commanders have such authority
that others follow because they have to.

Leaders show others what to do.
Commanders tell others what to do.

Leaders often start institutions.
Commanders often end institutions.

To determine if I am leading,
I need to look around.

If no one is following—I'm not one!
(Matthew 20:25–28)

...whoever wants to become great
among you must be your servant...
(Matthew 20:26)

Three

am I Jealous or Envious?

Jealousy
makes me want to keep from you
what is mine.

Envy
makes me want to get from you
what is yours.

Both can be fatal!
(Galatians 5:19–21)

The acts of the sinful nature
are obvious:...jealousy...envy...
(Galatians 5:19–21)

Four

am I Wise or Foolish?

God's wisdom
is foolishness to the world.

The world's wisdom
is foolishness to God.

Am I willing to be a *fool for Christ*
in the eyes of the world—

knowing that God is blessing me
and those around me with
His eternal wisdom and truth?
(1 Corinthians 1–3)

*Has not God made foolish
the wisdom of the world?*
(1 Corinthians 1:20)

217

Five

am I Optimistic or Realistic?

Optimism sees the glass half full.
Pessimism sees the glass half empty.

Realism sees the water in the glass.
(John 13:36–38)

Will you really lay down your life for me?
I tell you the truth,
before the rooster crows,
you will disown me three times!
(John 13:38)

Six

am I Asking or Arguing?

Two men asked Jesus the same question.

One was seeking an answer.
One was seeking an argument.

"Which one am I, Lord?"

Fortunately,
Jesus has answers for both!
(Luke 10:25–37, 18:18–25)

*...what must I do
to inherit eternal life?*
(Luke 10:25, 18:18)

Seven

am I Slave or Free?

God alone is totally free.

I am free
only as long as I stay within the limits
He has set forth.

Am I giving up my individual freedom
and following Jesus in this world—

In order to receive freedom in
His Kingdom forever?
(John 8:31–36)

So if the Son sets you free,
you will be free indeed.
(John 8:36)

Eight

am I Grateful or Thankful?

Gratitude
is a feeling I experience inwardly.

Thanks
is a fact I express outwardly.

The term "Gratitude" (Grateful)
occurs only three times in my Bible.

The term "Thank(s)"
occurs over 100 times.

When I am grateful, it helps me.
When I express thanks, it helps us both.
(Luke 17:7–19)

He threw himself at Jesus' feet
and thanked him—
and he was a Samaritan.
(Luke 17:16)

Nine

am I Lawful or Just?

Lawful is what is legal.
Just is what is right.

The law is necessary,
but it is not necessarily right.

Laws change from time to time
and are only as just as those in power.

We need man's law for order.
We need God for justice.

"Help me Lord, to be just—
not just lawful!"
(Luke 11:42; Romans 13:1–7)

…you give God a tenth…
but you neglect justice…
(Luke 11:42)

Ten

am I Forward or Backward?

When I was young, I looked forward
and thought it was my job to help bring
Heaven on Earth.

Now that I am old, I look backward
and realize
the world hasn't changed much.

God has made it clear
that my job is simply
to love God and to love people.

At the right time, Jesus will bring
Heaven on Earth.
(Matthew 6:9–10; Revelation 21–22)

*Then I saw a new heaven
and a new earth,
for the first heaven and the first earth
had passed away...*
(Revelation 21:1)

Eleven

am I Dead or Alive?

Death is the haunting question in life.

I can live for myself now,
but die forever when life is over.

Or I can die to myself now,
but live ever after.

The maxim is true:
Start hard—end easy!
Start easy—end hard!
(Matthew 16:24–26)

For whoever wants to save his life
will lose it,
but whoever loses his life for me
will find it.
(Matthew 16:25)

Twelve

am I Right or Wrong?

I used to believe
I was to try and make myself "right"
in this world,
so someday I could go to Heaven.

I was "wrong."
I can never make myself "right."

Instead, I am to believe in Jesus
and follow Him in this world.

When I do, He makes me "right."

And I will go to Heaven,
because of Him—not because of me!
(Romans 3:23, 6:23)

For the wages of sin is death,
but the gift of God is eternal life
in Christ Jesus our Lord.
(Romans 6:23)

Thirteen

am I Alien or Citizen?

There are two Kingdoms,
and they are opposed to one another.

I cannot be a citizen of both.

So I ask myself,

"Am I living as an 'alien and exile'
in the Kingdom of the World—

in exchange for eternal citizenship
in the Kingdom of God?"
(Hebrews 11:13–16)

*Instead they were longing
for a better country—
a heavenly one.*
(Hebrews 11:16)

Fourteen

am I Earning or Exploiting?

Earning entitles me to receive.
Exploiting enables me to receive.

When I work and create something of value,
I earn the right to payment.

When I buy something for less than it is worth
or sell it for more than it is worth,
I exploit value from others.

Earning builds trust.
Exploiting destroys trust.

Earning builds relationships.
Exploiting tears down relationships.

I wonder,
"am I earning or exploiting?"
(Proverbs 20:14; 2 Thessalonians 3:7–12)

"It's no good, it's no good!"
says the buyer; then off he goes
and boasts about his purchase.
(Proverbs 20:14)

Fifteen

am I Giving or Receiving?

The Bible says,
*"It is more blessed to give
than to receive."*

It is also more fun!

But giving puts us in control and
can build pride—

while receiving can be demeaning
but teach us humility.

Isn't it interesting that God
designed the world
so that we have to receive,
before we have anything to give?
(Acts 20:35; 1 Corinthians 4:7)

*What do you have
that you did not receive?*
(1 Corinthians 4:7)

Sixteen

am I Winning or Serving?

Competition and Winning have become
King and Queen in our world today.

However, the words "competition" and "winner"
do not even appear in my Bible.

Related terms such as
"compete" and "win(s)"
appear less than two dozen times.

By contrast, the terms "serve, service, serving, servant," etc.
appear over 1000 times.

It seems rather obvious which one
is most important to God.
(John 13:12–15)

*Now that I, your Lord and Teacher,
have washed your feet, you also
should wash one another's feet.*
(John 13:14)

Seventeen

am I Old or New?

"Love your neighbor as yourself"
is God's Old Commandment.

This is "contractual love"—
in which I am the standard.

"Love one another...
As I have loved you..."
is Jesus' New Commandment.

This is "sacrificial love"—
in which Jesus is the standard.

The old is good.
The new is best!
(Luke 10:25–28; John 13:34–35)

A new command I give you:
Love one another. As I have loved you,
so you must love one another.
(John 13:34)

Eighteen

am I Past, Present or Future?

Faith looks at the past and gives me
a foundation for life.

Hope looks at the future and
gives me a desire for life.

Love looks at the
past, present, and future,
and gives me a way of life.
(1Corinthians 13)

And now these three remain:
faith, hope, and love.
But the greatest of these is love.
(1 Corinthians 13:13)

Nineteen

am I Life Work or Legacy?

A Life Work is an objective in life.
A Legacy is a result of a Life Work.

Our Life Work
is to serve God's purpose
in our own generation.

Our Legacy will
pass on to following generations
how well we did it.
(Acts 13:36; Exodus 20:5–6, 34:5–7)

*For when David had served
God's purpose in his own generation,
he fell asleep...*
(Acts 13:36)

Twenty

am I Proud or Humble?

Pride is an emphasis on self.
Humility doesn't think of self.

Pride sees itself as superior.
Humility doesn't compare itself
with others.

Pride seeks power and position.
Humility seeks to serve others.

The Devil modeled pride.
Jesus modeled humility.

(A friend told me of a man
who received a button for his humility,
but they took it away when he wore it!)
(Isaiah 14:12–15; Philippians 2:1–11)

*Do nothing
out of selfish ambition or vain conceit,
but in humility
consider others better than yourselves.*
(Philippians 2:3)

Twenty-One

am I Interpreting or Inerrant?

I have little problem believing
that the Bible is

Inerrant

as originally delivered by God.

But I do become uneasy
when anyone suggests
their particular interpretation
or conclusion is also

Inerrant.
(Matthew 7:15–23)

Watch out for false prophets.
They come to you in sheep's clothing,
but inwardly they are ferocious wolves.
(Matthew 7:15)

Twenty-Two

am I Unity or Uniformity?

Unity is oneness in fact.
Uniformity is oneness in form.

Unity is voluntary.
Uniformity is forced.

Unity is from the power of love.
Uniformity is from the force of law.

The Bible speaks often of unity.
The Bible never mentions uniformity.

"Lord, I suppose we need some uniformity in life,
but help me seek unity whenever possible—
for myself and also for others!"
(Psalm 133; John 17:20–23)

How good and pleasant it is
when brothers live together in unity!
(Psalm 133:1)

Twenty-Three

am I Teaching or Preaching?

Teaching is explaining.
Preaching is proclaiming.

Teaching motivates us to think.
Preaching motivates us to act.

Teaching encourages us to know.
Preaching encourages us to do.

To have both
is a true gift from God.
(Colossians 1:28–29)

*We proclaim him,
admonishing and teaching everyone
with all wisdom...*
(Colossians 1:28)

Twenty-Four

am I Old or Young?

A young man said to me,
"Marvin, You're old!"

I smiled and answered,
"Yes—and it's OK, isn't it?"

Young is not good.
Old is not bad.

They simply are!
(Ecclesiastes 3:1–17)

There is a time for everything...
a time to be born and a time to die...
He has made everything
beautiful in its time...
(Ecclesiastes 3:1–2, 11)

Twenty-Five

am I Rich or Poor?

Nearly every major character
in the Old Testament
was rich, famous, or powerful.

By contrast, neither Jesus, nor any major character
in the New Testament,
had any worldly wealth, power, or position.

I keep asking myself,

"Am I giving up my right to everything in this world
and following Jesus into His Kingdom—

or am I clinging to the 'riches' in
the Kingdom of the World?"
(Matthew 6:19–33; Luke 12:16–21)

*You cannot serve
both God and Money.*
(Matthew 6:24)

Twenty-Six

am I Liking or Loving?

Liking someone
means I feel good.

Loving someone
means I act good.

And when I act good,
it usually helps me feel good.

Our granddaughter knew we needed both,
as she called to us each time we parted,

"I 'Wike' you, and I 'Wuv' you!"
(Ephesians 5:2; John 13:34–35)

*...and live a life of love, just as Christ loved us
and gave himself up for us...*
(Ephesians 5:2)

Twenty-Seven

am I Grace or Mercy?

Through grace,
I receive something good
I don't deserve.

Through mercy,
I don't receive something bad
I do deserve.

I am thankful that God's grace
will take me to Heaven—

and His mercy
will save me from Hell—

if

I believe and follow Him!
(Ephesians 2:4–9)

…God, who is rich in mercy, made us alive with Christ…
—it is by grace you have been saved…
(Ephesians 2:4–5)

Twenty-Eight

am I Believing or Knowing?

The Apostle John wrote his Gospel
so we may believe *Jesus is the Christ*
and have *life in His name.*

He wrote the book of 1 John
so those who believe may know
they *have eternal life.*

I have come to understand
that I can't know
what God is telling me,

until I believe
in Him and His Son.
(John 20:31; 1 John 5:13–20)

*We know also that the Son of God has come,
and has given us understanding...*
(I John 5:20)

Twenty-Nine

am I Form or Substance?

Form is like a bucket that carries water.
Substance is the water in the bucket.

If we lose the bucket,
the water is poured out onto the sand
and disappears.

If we lose the water, we die of thirst.

I wonder where the world
would be today

if God had not given
His water to His saints?

And, if His saints had not placed His water
in the bucket we call the Bible?
(John 7:38; 2 Timothy 3:16–17)

Whoever believes in me, as the Scripture has said,
streams of living water will flow from within him.
(John 7:38)

Thirty

am I Loved or Admired?

Others love us,
when they experience
love from us.

Others admire us,
when they witness us do
something extraordinarily well.

As I grow older, I realize more and more,
I would rather be loved than admired!
(1 John 4:19)

We love because He first loved us.
(1 John 4:19)

Thirty-One

am I Being or Doing?

If I am in control,
I try and "do" in order to "be."
That builds pride.

If God is in control,
He causes me to "be" in order to "do."
That builds humility.

I have concluded
"Who I am"
and
"Whose I am"
are more important
than what I try to accomplish.

(As I once heard someone say,
"If who I am is what I do,
then when I don't, I'm not!")
(Galatians 2:20; Ephesians 2:8–10)

*…I no longer live,
but Christ lives in me…*
(Galatians 2:20)

Conclusion

The statements you have been reading have been helpful to me. I thank God for allowing me to write them. I sincerely hope they will encourage you to think and pray and receive what He has for you.

But they are still simply one old man's thoughts and conclusions—and they are only as true as they agree with God and His Word.

About 3000 years ago, another old man (believed to be King Solomon) wrote the Book of Ecclesiastes. He looked back on his life of wealth, power, prestige, and pleasure and called it "chasing the wind." At the end, after having it all, he concluded:

> *Now all has been heard;*
> *here is the conclusion of the matter:*
> *Fear God and keep his commandments,*
> *for this is the whole duty of man.*
> (Ecclesiastes 12:13)

So I pray you will go directly to *"I AM"* and His Word for the pure answers to all your questions.

May God Eternally Bless You
As You Follow Him!

Part VIII

Looking Forward With Hope!

And hope does not disappoint us,
because God has poured out His love into our hearts
by the Holy Spirit, whom He has given us.
(Romans 5:5)

Preface

2012

During the Civil War, President Lincoln opened his legendary Gettysburg Address with the memorable phrase:

"Four score and seven years ago…"

As I prepared to celebrate my 87th birthday a few weeks ago, I realized that I, too, have reached the age of "four score and seven" years. And it somewhat sobered me to recognize that I have lived as long as from the beginning of our nation to the Civil War!

Each season of life has brought new challenges and new rewards. Born in the 1920s, the era of post-World War I excitement culminating in the Stock Market crash of 1929, my boyhood was spent in the difficult years of the drought and economic disaster of the Great Depression in the 1930s.

The 1940s found us attempting to bring peace and stability to the world by defeating the dictatorships of Germany, Italy, and Japan. We won, but troubles didn't end and utopia didn't arrive. Instead America immersed itself for the decades of the 1950s, 1960s, 1970s, and most of the 1980s in trying to contain the threat of Communism all over the world in what we have come to know as the Cold War.

The 1990s found us beginning a new Information Age with "economic exuberance" and hopes for a bright new 21st century— only to find our expectations were short lived as we experienced the new challenge of Islamic radicalism and the War against Terror with the attacks on September 11, 2001.

However, in looking back it is clear to me that the great national and international problems we experienced are not the main thrust of my memories. Instead, I recall a boyhood working on our little farm surrounded by the love of our family and friends and teachers. World War II was a time for adventure and manhood. The Cold War era brought college and love and marriage and children and friends, followed by years in the work world and the opportunity to grow ever closer to Jesus and the brothers and sisters in His Kingdom. And my more recent years in this new century are full of personal relationships—not national or international problems!

In summary, I have found that life, like politics, is primarily local! We *talk* about the weather and big problems most of us can do little about. But we *live* and are *eternally affected* by people and events that surround us each and every day!

When we are young, many of us believe our generation can change the world and make it right. But when we near the end, we know we didn't. And we never will, because an imperfect mankind cannot fix itself.

As I reach the ripe old age of four score and seven years, I now read Ecclesiastes with a sense of comradeship, rather than discouragement, and I recognize there truly is "a time for everything" and that God "has made everything beautiful in its time" (Ecclesiastes 3).

I have concluded my job is not to fix the world. Rather it is to be who God has created me to be, and then (like King David) allow Him to use me to "serve His purpose in (my) own generation" (Acts 13:36).

This autumn we are engaging in an historic national election. The consequences are important and will have serious effects for many years to come. But when we put these events in perspective, we realize they are no more challenging than those our people have faced in the past. More importantly, as we read the Bible, it is quickly apparent that we in America in the year 2012 are not facing anything worse than people have faced since the beginning of time.

This past summer, we took several weeks off from our normal schedule to spend time in Colorado. While we were away, we listened and read the daily (and sometimes hourly) news reports. It didn't take long to become discouraged. Fortunately, while we were gone I also felt the urge to review some of my previously unpublished work. As I reread *Looking Forward With Hope* (originally written about the time we prepared to enter this new century), I saw God's light shining through the clouds.

And as I reread the scripture references about Hope, I also realized how much this theme has rung consistently through God's Word. I do not believe it is any coincidence that the Bible ends in Hope (*Revelation*) and that so many books of the Bible also end in Hope. No matter how bad or how dark the circumstances that surround us, God is telling us today, as in the past, that He is with us!

I decided now is a good time to share this booklet with you. I pray it is helpful. But remember, we all err, so hold on to what is good (of God)—and discard the rest.

From Grandpa With Love

Looking Forward With Hope!

Introduction

Our view of both the past and the future vitally affect how we feel and how we live. Unfortunately, many of us believe that time really begins when we are born and ends when we die! And because of our finite minds, we often seem able to conceptualize ahead only as far as we can actually see behind.

One result of this limitation is that it can cause our view of life to expand, and then to contract, as we move across the years. For example: at age 10, we see ahead ten years to about age 20. At age 20, we can conceive of (although not really comprehend) the twenty years that stretch ahead to age 40. And at age 40, we are often startled as we look forty years forward and realize that at the end of those forty years, our life will be at or near its end.

Then an interesting, but debilitating, concept often seems to occur. Instead of continuing to expand our view of life forward to as many years as we have already lived, we may begin to contract our view forward to only as many years as we believe we have left to live.

For example, by age 50 we may now look ahead only thrity-five years to age 85. And although by age 70 we may have mentally increased our expectancy to age 90, we now narrow our view forward to only twenty years!

Thus, as we reach our middle years, life can begin to crowd inward upon us, and we watch the end approaching ever more closely. The result can be that we become frustrated, depressed, or even bitter. We find that time is running out, and we are increasingly living in memories of the past—while the sun goes down on our view of the future.

I decided that approach is a terrible waste. If I am able to see and learn from the increasing number of years behind me, it seems more logical to use that hindsight to look forward and extrapolate what we have learned to an ever-expanding and exciting lifespan ahead. And, if we apply that same concept to history, we are able to look backward far before we were born, and perhaps see ahead (although dimly) far beyond our own death.

The result for me has been that expanding my view of the past helps me better understand the few years of my life. It also gives me a desire to look forward with hope for my generation and the generations that are to come, and on into eternity, particularly when I view the past, the present, and the future through the pages of God's Word, the Bible.

As I thought about this subject, I began to search for Biblical characters whose lives and insights from God might instruct me how better to look forward, both in this life and on into eternity. Let me pass on to you some of what I found in the hope it may also help you.

Looking Forward in This Life

First let's talk about looking forward in this life. I found the first decision I needed to make was whether I wanted to be a

"Hezekiah" or a "Jeremiah." God used both of these men mightily during their lifetimes, but it was Jeremiah who reflected a heart for future generations.

Hezekiah

King Hezekiah was a colorful and capable ruler. After years of faithful service, he became ill and "at the point of death." God heard his plea and granted him fifteen additional years of life (Isaiah 38:6). Unfortunately, after his return to health, Hezekiah's pride apparently caused him to display his kingdom's wealth and treasures to some visiting Babylonians. When the prophet Isaiah learned of Hezekiah's foolish actions, he told the king:

> *Hear the word of the Lord Almighty: The time will surely come when everything in your palace, and all that your fathers have stored up until this day, will be carried off to Babylon.*
> *Nothing will be left, says the Lord. And some of your own descendants, your own flesh and blood who will be born to you, will be taken away, and they will become eunuchs in the palace of the king of Babylon.*
> (Isaiah 39:5–7)

How sad it is then to read Hezekiah's shortsighted reply:

> *"The word of the Lord you have spoken is good," Hezekiah replied. For he thought, "There will be peace and security in **my** lifetime."*
> (Isaiah 39:8, emphasis added)

Here was a man who had limited his view of the future only to the end of his own life, apparently without much thought or concern for those who would follow him. Tragically, he seemed content to allow his hope to die with him.

As I read further, I read with even greater sadness the story of Hezekiah's son who ruled Jerusalem for fifty-five years after Hezekiah's death. The Bible records how Manasseh apparently abandoned all hope and trust in God and "did evil in the sight of the Lord" by following pagan gods and "detestable practices" (2 Kings 21:1–18). Here it also records the gruesome actions of this son who succeeded Hezekiah:

> *Moreover, Manasseh also shed so much innocent blood*
> *that he filled Jerusalem from end to end—*
> *beside the sin that he had caused Judah to commit,*
> *so that they did evil in the eyes of the Lord.*
> (2 Kings 21:16)

Fortunately, Manasseh later returned to the Lord, but only after his enemies…

> *took Manasseh prisoner, put a hook in his nose,*
> *bound him with bronze shackles, and took him to Babylon.*
> (2 Chronicles 33:11b)

As I read of this great tragedy, I could not help wondering how much different Manasseh's life and the lives of his people might have been, if his father, Hezekiah, had looked forward beyond his own lifetime and encouraged his son to look forward, with trust and hope in God to help them prepare for and weather the storm of war that was approaching.

I am convinced that we need hope about the future for ourselves, but we also need to give hope to those who follow us. Dr. Elton Trueblood stated it well at page 58 of his book *The Life We Prize*:

> A man has made at least a start on discovering the meaning of human life when he plants shade trees under which he knows full well he will never sit.

If we look only to the end of our lifetime, we rob ourselves, those around us, and those who follow us of the hope we need to be God's people in a sordid and dying world.

Jeremiah

Now let's look at the prophet Jeremiah, who lived during the Babylonian conquest and Jewish exile foretold by Isaiah. Jerusalem was under siege by the Babylonians, but God promised Jeremiah that the Jews would return to Jerusalem after seventy years of captivity, and also gave hope for the intervening hard times:

> *This is what the Lord says:*
> *"When seventy years are completed for Babylon,*
> *I will come to you and fulfill my gracious promise*
> *to bring you back to this place.*
> *For I know the plans I have for you", declares the Lord,*
> *"plans to prosper you and not to harm you,*
> *plans to give you hope and a future."*
> (Jeremiah 29:10-11)

Acting on God's instructions, and looking forward seventy years, Jeremiah bought a field and had the deed preserved for future generations (Jeremiah 32:6–15). And for seventy years the Jewish exiles were strengthened by Jeremiah's long view forward. When the seventy years were over, the people did return to Jerusalem, as recorded in the Old Testament books of Ezra and Nehemiah.

When I saw the contrast between these two views of life, I decided I wanted to be a "Jeremiah" and not a "Hezekiah." As I searched further, I found there were many more examples of Biblical characters who looked a long way forward, some many more years ahead than Jeremiah. For example:

Joseph

Joseph was the son of Jacob (later known as Israel), the grandson of Isaac, and the great-grandson of Abraham. It was Joseph who was sold into Egyptian slavery by his envious brothers (Genesis 37:19–28), and it was Joseph whom God delivered out of slavery and made second only to Pharaoh (Genesis 41:39–40). Later, Joseph reconciled with his brothers and brought them and their father to live in Egypt. Many years later, as Joseph was dying, he gave instructions that his bones were to be taken back "to the land He (God) promised on oath to Abraham, Isaac, and Jacob" (Genesis 50:24–25).

As I pondered this account, I also noted that God had earlier revealed to Joseph's great-grandfather, Abraham, that the Jews' enslavement in Egypt would last 400 years (Genesis 15:13). Suddenly I realized that when Joseph gave his deathbed instructions, he was looking forward nearly 400 years to the time Moses would lead the Israelites out of Egypt and back into the "promised land"!

For 400 years, the Jews were sustained through their Egyptian bondage with God's promise to Abraham, and Joseph's reliance on that promise to insist that his bones be taken back to the "promised land." We have no way of knowing how much Moses was strengthened in his historic journey by the faith displayed by Joseph. But we do know that Moses records this passage at the start of their journey out of enslavement in Egypt:

> *Moses took the bones of Joseph with him because Joseph had made*
> *the sons of Israel swear on oath. He had said,*
> *"God will surely come to your aid,*
> *and then you must carry my bones up with you from this place."*
> (Exodus 13:19)

Just as God promised Jeremiah that He would bring the Jews out of Babylonian exile after seventy years of captivity, so had He also promised Abraham that He would bring the Jews out of Egyptian captivity after 400 years. In each case the people looked with hope far beyond their own lives and trusted God to do as He had promised—and He did!

Isaiah

Next, let's look again at the prophet Isaiah. Not only did Isaiah prophesy to King Hezekiah about the Babylonian invasion that would take place in a few years, but he also foretold much about the coming of Jesus, the Messiah (e.g., Isaiah 53), that would not happen until some 750 years later!

Century after century the Jews clung to the hope that their Messiah would come. Despite foreign conquests and the difficulties of their life, they always looked forward—not knowing when it would happen, but faithfully trusting God to keep His promise. A hope that was still bright when Jesus was born in Bethlehem (e.g., Luke 2:25–38).

Jesus

Most significant of all the Biblical figures who looked a long way forward was Jesus Himself, as He predicted His own return to earth that would follow His death and resurrection. While He stated, "No one knows about that day or hour..." (Matthew 24:36), we now know He was looking ahead at least 2000 years!

For 2000 years believers have watched and waited for Jesus' second coming. It has been said that every generation believes His return may happen in their lifetime. Perhaps God planned it that way so we would live in expectancy. In addition, older people often seem to think *the* end time is near as *their* end time approaches. In any case, this hope has been kept alive for 20 centuries.

But, as wonderful as this event will be, it also poses a dilemma since it drastically shortens our view of the future if we believe that Jesus return is eminent. It behooves us, of course, to look for Him at any moment. However, we have to realize it may be *another* 2000 years before He comes. Because of that we need to have a sort of bifocal vision, looking for His immediate return, but also living as if such return could be delayed for many, many years. Otherwise, we can be like the church at Thessalonica that suffered from this desire. The Apostle Paul, in his first letter to these believers, (1 Thessalonians) discussed Jesus' return. Apparently, he then found it necessary to write a second letter (2 Thessalonians) and admonish them not to sit and wait, but rather to work and get on with life. So should we!

Let me say again that I am not a prophet. I don't have any message from God leading me to believe that I should look forward any specific number of days or years. But I do believe that I should look at least as far ahead as I have already lived. Since I am 87 years old, I am now pushing my time horizon for earthly events to the year 2099! What a challenge it is to think about my great-grandchildren reaching age 87! It totally changes my perspective from thinking only about the few years I may have to live. I encourage each of you to consider this question for yourselves and decide how far forward you want to look.

Jesus said we do not know the "day or hour" of His return. Neither do we know when He may call *us* home. I believe, therefore, we should follow His instructions to watch carefully for His return (Matthew 24:42), but also do the work He has given us (Matthew 24:45–46), including looking forward as far as we are able, as long as we are able.

Of one thing we can be certain: God has watched over and provided for us all the days of our lives to date, so we can be confident He will continue to do so for the rest of our days. And when we look at the history of the Bible, we can see that He has watched over and provided for all those who have followed Him over the centuries, So we can live in complete trust and hope for our children, our grandchildren, our great-grandchildren, and all the generations who submit to and follow Him in the future!

No matter what circumstances may happen, whether good or bad, God is in control, and we can rely on His promises. Hallelujah!

Looking Forward Into Eternity

Up to this point, we have been discussing looking forward in this life. Now let's talk about looking forward into eternity.

Life After Death
The first question we have to ask ourselves is whether or not there is such a thing as existence after this life. To use the phraseology of an old mentor of mine, "The answer for any thinking person must be, 'Yes'".

People across the ages show evidence of belief in life after death. And they have often come to this conclusion independently and without consultation with other societies. Even a casual look at life, with all its beauty and orderliness, cries out that it was created, and not an accident.

"Someone" beyond this physical universe as we know it must have brought it all into existence. The writers of the Declaration of Independence were not unique when they spoke of our being "endowed by our Creator." The real question we need to ask ourselves is not,

"Is there life after death?"

But rather,

"Where and how am I going to spend eternity?"

The Bible makes it clear that there is an eternity, and that we have the option where and how we choose to spend it. For some it will mean unspeakable joy and eternal life with God and His family in what the Bible calls Heaven. For others it will mean a place of torment and eternal separation from God in what the Bible calls Hell (Luke 16:23).

What Must We Do to Have Eternal Life With God?
Obviously, if there is eternal life with God, we want to know how to have it. Perhaps the simplest answer is found in the oft-quoted verse found in John 3:16:

> *For God so loved the world that He gave His one and only Son,*
> *that whoever believes in Him shall not perish*
> *but have eternal life.*

This decision can be made by anyone at any time before we die, as illustrated by the following conversation between Jesus, as He hung dying on the cross, and a thief being crucified nearby:

> *Then he* (the thief) *said, "Jesus, remember me when you*
> *come into your kingdom." Jesus answered him,*
> *"I tell you the truth, today you will be with me in paradise."*
> (Luke 23:42–43)

A New Body

Some of the ancients believed we would travel into the next world with our physical bodies, so they prepared the dead for travel and even supplied food and other necessaries in the burial process. While the Bible speaks of the "resurrection of the dead," it makes it clear that we will have a different body than we have known here on earth (1 Corinthians 15).

Because of Adam's original sin and our sinful nature, we are always subject to death and decay in this world. But not so the new body that we will receive. The Apostle Paul phrases it this way:

So will it be with the resurrection of the dead.
The body that is sown is perishable,
it is raised imperishable; it is sown in dishonor, it is raised in glory;
it is sown in weakness,
it is raised in power; it is sown a natural body,
it is raised a spiritual body.
(I Corinthians 15:42–44a)

No more pain, no more physical or mental defects, no more deterioration as we age—only a perfect body for a perfect eternity. That, too, is a Hallelujah!

What Will Heaven Be Like?

The more we read and study and think on these Biblical references to Heaven (e.g., Revelation 21–22), the more we begin to look forward with hope and joy to being there. For example:

- There will be no death or sorrow or unhappiness in Heaven.
- There we will worship and serve the Lord.
- There will never again be darkness or night because there will always be the radiance of God for light.
- And perhaps, best of all, all believers will be together with Jesus and other believers forever!

No wonder countless believers over the centuries have been willing to give up everything in this present life, in order that they might share in this new life after death. No one has said it more eloquently than the Apostle Paul in his letter to the Philippians:

*I want to know Christ and the power of his resurrection
and the fellowship of sharing in his sufferings,
becoming like him in his death, and so, somehow,
to attain to the resurrection from the dead."*
(Philippians 3:10–11)

Conclusion

Let me close by offering a prayer for the future:

First, that we will all look further and further forward in this life, the older we become, rather than being boxed in by our own brief life span.

Second, that we will seek the benefit of those who follow us at least to the 3rd and 4th generation, in the hope that all our physical and spiritual children, grandchildren and great-grandchildren will all learn to walk with God.

And, finally, that we will all look forward with anticipation and joy to the eternal life God has planned for us, a life that we will experience forever with Him and all the other believers in a perfect new place that will be immeasurably better than we could ever have imagined!

Thanks for listening.

God Bless You All!

Epilogue

The following words were written in 1991 as an epilogue for Part I, "What Am I Missing?" They now seem a fitting ending for our entire book about *Passing It On*.

***

Many years ago, I read with admiration the letter of a young man in his 30s who was approaching death by cancer. In this letter to his son, he carefully detailed qualities and observations that he encouraged his boy to consider and to emulate. What a wonderful legacy!

Recently, a longtime friend told me that he had learned he has only a few months to live. "I am so grateful that I know," he said. "I have always worried that I would die unexpectedly." At first, this seemed an unusual statement, but gradually I have seen the maturity of his wisdom as he was able to put his house in order before he passed away.

Unfortunately, not all of us will have the luxury of knowing when we will die. However, we all know in advance that we will die, so we should act accordingly. Let's pass on the message of salvation and the other teachings of the Bible. As the Psalmist says:

> *He decreed statutes for Jacob and established the law in Israel,*
> *which he commanded our forefathers to teach their children,*
> *so the next generation would know them,*
> *even the children yet to be born,*
> *and they in turn would tell their children.*
> *Then they would put their trust in God*

and would not forget his deeds but would keep his commands.
(Psalm 78:5–7)

Last Wills and Testaments, Trusts, and Living Wills are obviously important considerations. But in a more narrow and personal way, so are the teachings of each of our lives. I encourage you, therefore, to consider your life and write down what has been important to you that you don't want the next generation(s) to miss.

Let's pass on all that we can to make life richer, fuller, and more abundant for those who follow us.

***

A Closing Thank-You

I was born on August 10, 1925. One of my earliest memories was eating angel-food cake and then leaving for Yellowstone National Park on my 5th birthday on August 10, 1930. I celebrated my 20th birthday on August 10, 1945 on the island of Guam just four days before we completed the last air bombing raid against Japan in World War II. I surrendered my life to Christ and was "born again" spiritually at the age of 44, on August 10, 1969. Other birthdays are rich with memories that marked my life.

Now, as I approach Age 90 on August 10, 2015, I thank God for enabling me to complete these five volumes *"From Grandpa With Love"* to try and convey what He has been teaching me about *Life*:

> Volume I *"Four Generations"*, walked through an 85 year *Journey Through Life*.
> Volume II *"Faith"*, discussed the need for *A Foundation for Life*.
> Volume III *"Marriage"*, conveyed some lessons from 60 years of *Sharing Life*.
> Volume IV *"Vocation"*, focused on *Our Life Work*.
> Volume V *"Passing It On"*, emphasized the importance of *Investing In Lives*.

I am deeply indebted to all of you who encouraged me and helped me get it done. Without you these books might never have been born. You have my profound gratitude and thanks!

Finally, I thank each of you who read any or all of the books. I know it is not easy to digest the breadth and depth of over 1000 pages about *Life*, but I pray it is worthwhile.

What I have set forth has been out of thanksgiving and love to God and all of you. It has been my earnest desire to give you truth as I have seen it. If that is accomplished, it will be a valuable inheritance—so take it with my blessing!

Hopefully, there will be more times during the days and years ahead, when you, or other readers, can take these books off the shelf and relive some of these experiences and conclusions that will prove to be meaningful and helpful. But remember, we all err, so read carefully, consult the Bible and Godly counsel, and then hold on to what is good (of God)—and discard the rest.

To Him Be the Glory!

From Grandpa With Love

"As for me, this is my covenant with them," says the Lord.
"My Spirit, who is on you,
and my words that I have put in your mouth
will not depart from your mouth, or from the mouths of your children,
or from the mouths of their descendants
from this time on and forever," says the Lord.
(Isaiah 59:21)

270